DATE DUE

NA7238.B3B76 1988   6289

BROWER
DESIGN IN FAMILIAR PLACES:
WHAT MAKES HOME ENVIRONMEN

DATE DUE			

DESIGN

IN FAMILIAR
PLACES

Cover design is a detail from ADORATION OF THE HOME, 1921–22
Grant Wood
Oil on canvas, 22 3/4 × 81 3/8 in.
© Cedar Rapids Museum of Art, Private Collection

DESIGN
IN FAMILIAR
PLACES

What Makes Home Environments
Look Good

SIDNEY BROWER

PRAEGER

New York
Westport, Connecticut
London

Copyright Acknowledgment

The author and the publisher are grateful to the following for granting the use of:

Lyrics from GIGI by Alan Jay Lerner and Frederick Loewe, Copyright © 1957, 1958 by Chappell & Co., Inc.
Copyright renewed. International copyright secured. All rights reserved. Used by permission.

Library of Congress Cataloging-in-Publication Data

Brower, Sidney N.
    Design in familiar places : what makes home environments look good/
    Sidney Brower.
       p.   cm.
    Bibliography: p.
    Includes index.
    ISBN 0-275-92686-9 (alk. paper)
    1. Architecture, Domestic—Maryland—Baltimore. 2. Architecture—
Environmental aspects—Maryland—Baltimore. 3. Architecture—
Maryland—Baltimore—Human factors. 4. Baltimore (Maryland)—
Buildings, structures, etc. 5. Architecture, Domestic—Philosophy.
6. Architectural design. I. Title.
NA7238.B3B76   1988   87-27889
728—dc19

Library of Congress Catalog Card Number: 87-27889
ISBN: 0-275-92686-9

First published in 1988

Praeger Publishers, One Madison Avenue, New York, NY 10010
A division of Greenwood Press, Inc.

Printed in the United States of America

The paper used in this book complies with the
Permanent Paper Standard issued by the National
Information Standards Organization (Z39.48-1984).

10 9 8 7 6 5 4 3 2 1

For Cynthia, Kate, and Gideon

Contents

Illustrations

FIGURES

TABLES

Preface

This is a book about residential environments: what makes them look good, and what makes us use them and care for them the way we do. The subject is not houses or services, but rather the residents themselves: how their attitudes, perceptions, and behaviors change the definition of housing quality and the nature of the design problem in residential areas. Four personal anecdotes illustrate the issues to be addressed.

In the mid-1960s I worked on a plan to eliminate blighted housing in Baltimore. (The idea that one can use a plant disease as an analogy for poor housing is an example of the simple-minded thinking that sometimes masquerades as theory—but that is another topic.) We were in the process of testing an evaluation form for rating housing quality, a checklist of items to look for (such as sagging beams, bowing walls, rotting window frames, and peeling paint) with a rating scale for each item that ranged from *very good* to *very poor*. We came across a street where the houses were in dreadful shape. They deserved a *very poor* rating on all counts. Most of the houses were abandoned, but in the middle of the block one house was occupied. The windows were clean, and there were fresh curtains and well-tended flowerboxes. In the midst of desolation the house was cozy and cheerful. As a structure it looked no better than its neighbors, but as housing it did not look nearly as bad. It seemed to warrant a higher rating and so we introduced a new item on the checklist: a rating for visible improvements that could be attributed to the occupant.

———

I worked in a neighborhood where residents complained that the local playgrounds were being vandalized, littered, and used by undesirables. When we looked into the matter we discovered that one playground had far fewer problems than the others, and it was in much better shape. We found that a resident whose house abutted this playground had taken a proprietary interest in it: she watched over it and intervened energetically when people used it in a way that she felt was inappropriate. She had gone so far as to install in her yard a floodlight that was trained on the playground, and at night potential troublemakers would find themselves suddenly illuminated, and berated by the lady herself. The local people knew that if you were going to get into mischief, this was not the place to do it. The solution to the playground's problems had nothing to do with physical design.

I accompanied a group of officials to inspect a program in which vacant houses were being rehabilitated for sale to low-income families. We visited a house that had just been completed. The occupants had not yet moved in. The interior walls of the house had been rebuilt, and redecorated in bright colors. There were new doors and windows and a modern bathroom and kitchen. The rooms were light and airy. There was no doubt but that this was a decent house. But looking through the front windows one looked at houses in need of maintenance and repair, graffitti-covered walls, broken windows, and litter blowing in the wind. The prospect from the back windows was even more dismal. I found myself wondering whether the housing conditions would have been worse if the house had been less "well-designed" and the people in the neighborhood had been more in control of their environment. The new residents of this house would have to be determined indeed to prevail against the neighborhood tolerance for vandalism and neglect.

There was a meeting of low-income residents to discuss the housing provisions of a new plan for their area and I was there as a planner for the city to speak about the importance of good design. As a caution, I showed several slides of a long, barrack-like block of row houses that had been completed a year or so previously in another part of the city. Each unit had a row of steps, two yew trees, and a neoclassical plaster surround to the front door. The buildings had no architectural distinction whatsoever. I showed it to make the point that while the community needed new housing, it should not settle for something like *that.* I am not sure what I expected when the slides appeared on the screen; perhaps a general gasp of horror. Instead, a man in the audience said, "We can never afford places as good as this." He obviously thought the houses were attractive, and judging by the murmurs from around the room, many of those present agreed with him.

I realized that my audience and I were seeing different things. I saw ordinary, unfashionable, inexpensive houses, with awkward proportions, mediocre workmanship, and little attention to detail. The residents saw new housing, in good condition, clean and tidy and not marked by vandalism; and they concluded that this was a place where the residents were respectable, caring, and safe. What I perceived as inadequate, they saw as highly desirable. With a middle-income audience I might have pressed the point that the houses were not well designed, but I suspected that a low-income audience might have ideas about design that were different from my own. I was accustomed to evaluate design by the way it affected me. Perhaps I needed to look at the way that it affected them.

I tell these anecdotes to illustrate the point that houses and services, important as they are, do not fully account for residential satisfaction. Good housing is not merely a matter of designing good houses and a good service delivery system. To create good housing we must create places that people care about and that satisfy their need for familiar surroundings. These two ideas—care and familiarity—are interwoven themes in this book.

Of all the places that we use in the course of our everyday lives there are probably none that we know as well as the residential area that we call home, and because we are so familiar with it we see it in a special way. Outsiders (that is, people who do not live there and are just visiting) do not see it in this way, and designers (who are by necessity strangers in most of the places they design) tend to see it as outsiders. Residents respond to things that outsiders are not even aware of and they ignore things that strike outsiders as important, and when the two groups evaluate the environment they use different values and priorities. It follows that if we are to improve the way a residential environment looks to its residents we must take a resident's viewpoint and see it through familiar eyes.

Even if there were places as familiar as our home environment we would not care for them in the same way. Home environments are special, and their power to evoke feelings extends beyond their intrinsic physical qualities. Objects are seen not only for themselves, but for the information they contain about the identity, circumstances, and social relationships of the people who made them, and who own and use them. Designers sometimes believe that resident care is a natural consequence of living in good architecture, but it is not so. Residents see architecture in a social context, and when they do not feel accountable for their environment, they are less likely to care for it. In such cases, designers must go beyond the traditional range of design concerns. This may involve restricting access, providing opportunities for surveillance, developing an organization to manage shared spaces, stimulating feelings of pride and responsibility, supporting and rewarding acts of care, and discouraging and punishing acts of vandalism and neglect. These are not traditional areas of design concern.

The book is divided into two sections. The first section is a development of general ideas: the environment can be seen in different ways, residents do not see their home environment as outsiders do, this has direct implications for design theory and practice, it widens the area of the designers' concerns, and it leads them into unfamiliar fields of activity.

The second section of the book consists of case studies that I have been associated with, that support the ideas developed earlier and illustrate their application in one type of residential environment. These case studies involve a systematic look at residents' perceptions, attitudes, and behaviors. My training in physical design hardly equipped me for this kind of research and I owe a special debt of gratitude to my colleagues, especially Penny Williamson, Richard Chase, Ralph Taylor, Stephen Gottfredson, Peggy Latimer, Edward Wood, and Roger Stough.

A book that deals with design and perception straddles the fields of the arts and the social and behavioral sciences. This creates special problems for a writer. Artists prefer information in a form that they can respond to intuitively, that is qualitative, diffuse, and ambiguous enough to allow for individual interpretation. Scientists, on the other hand, prefer information to be logical, quantitative, and conclusive. Artists are most interested in things that spark their imagination and scientists in things that satisfy their curiosity. Artists are dissatisfied if the major ideas are not supported by images (how does one show a picture of a familiar place?). Scientists are dissatisfied if ideas are not supported by data, but artists are put off by charts and tables. I have tried to skirt these difficulties by writing for the general reader. I use colloquial rather than formal language, meaning that I gloss over distinctions between concepts like perception and conception, and I use "look," "appear," "see," and "perceive" as if they mean the same thing. In the interests of readability much of the commentary is relegated to end notes and readers are referred to outside sources for supporting data.

Various sections of this book have appeared in slightly different form as: "Planners in the neighborhood: A cautionary tale," in R. B. Taylor (ed.), *Urban Neighborhoods: Research and Policy,* New York: Praeger, 1986; "Home and new-home territories," in Altman and Werner (eds.), *Home Environment: Advances in Theory and Research,* New York: Plenum, 1985; "Residents' perceptions of territorial features and perceived local threat," with Kathleen Dockett and Ralph B. Taylor, in *Environment and Behavior* 15, no. 4 (Sage, July 1983): 419–37; "Territory in urban settings," in Altman, Rapoport, and Wohlwill (eds.), *Human Behavior and Environment, Advances in Theory and Research* 4, *Environment and Culture,* New York: Plenum, 1980; "Tools, Toys, Masterpieces, Mediums," in *Landscape* 19, no. 2 (January 1975): 28–32; "Outdoor recreation as a function of the urban housing environment," with Penelope Williamson, in *Environment and Behavior* 6, no. 3 (Sage, September 1974): 295–345; "The signs we learn to read," in *Landscape* 15, no. 1 (Autumn 1965): 9–12.

It is hard to say where one's ideas come from when there are so many influences, but two sources are easy to identify: Kevin Lynch and Donald Appleyard, who taught me to look. Most of my studies were done for or in conjunction with the Baltimore City Department of Planning directed by Larry Reich. The studies were funded by the City of Baltimore, and through grants from several agencies of the U.S. Government: the Department of Housing and Urban Development, National Institutes of Health, Department of Justice, Department of the Interior, and the National Endowment for the Arts. I am grateful for their support. I am also grateful to the many residents of Baltimore who met with us, answered our questions, and filled in our forms with such patience and friendliness. I am grateful to Cynthia Brower for the cover design. Finally, I am grateful to the School of Social Work and Community Planning and the University of Maryland for having given me the time and support to work on this book.

Part I

1

Three Faces of Design

One can look at the environment in different ways, and each way recommends its own set of design concerns and purposes.

Several years ago I attended a conference in Barcelona, Spain. The last meetings of the conference took place on Wednesday, and my charter flight back to the States did not leave until the following Tuesday. I had time on my hands. On the way, I had flown over the Straits of Gibraltar and had been amazed to see how narrow they were. Morocco had never seemed so accessible.

My image of Morocco was not Bergman and Bogart; it was old walled towns, white buildings, narrow winding streets, minarets, oriental rugs, patterned tiles, and women in veils. It was exotic, different, unspoiled. It was getting back to the basics of design.

You must go to Fez, they said, and a friend in Barcelona gave me the name of a hotel there. When I arrived it was night, and seen through the taxicab window the city was dark and fragmented.

In the morning I saw that I was on a hill that overlooked a broad, shallow, river basin. Far below the hotel lay the *medina*, contained within its walls. Minarets pierced the dense geometry of whites and greys that changed with the shifting sun. Lines of men and women, some in dark and some in white robes, picked their way down the hillside toward the city gates. Fez promised to be everything that I had hoped for and expected.

Quite early that morning, a cab deposited me at the medina wall. I had engaged a guide, an elderly man, and I followed him through the gate and then along a narrow path that branched and branched again. We turned left, then right, then left and left again. In a short time I had completely lost my bearings.

We twisted through a maze of narrow streets; some seemed no more than six feet wide, and none wider than fifteen. They were lined with unbroken street walls, plastered and weatherstained, punctuated here and there with small screened windows, and doorways leading to dark courtyards and narrow stairs curving upward. At the end of a street there was an opening with intricately carved surround and multicolored tiles, and a view into a mosque, with layers of arcaded archways leading back to a sunlit inner courtyard; the interior was dim and cool, with brightly colored carpets, perforated screens, and ornate iron lamps.

Walking along, I was not aware of individual buildings, but of a solid architectural mass through which the streets had been gouged and burrowed. Here and there fountains were set into the street wall, and water spilled into shallow containers, tile-backed with bright, geometric designs. Vistas unfolded and opened and then closed again.

In the *souk,* reed screens roofed over the street, casting complicated light patterns on displays of bread, fruit, vegetables, meat, dates, herbs, cakes, baskets, shoes, and cloth. Flies buzzed around a table loaded with *halvah.* Merchants sat in small compartments, completely open to the street. I could see tailors sitting crosslegged, and bakers stoking their ovens. Pack donkeys moved slowly through the crowds and people made way for them.

In a dark corner, a beggarwoman squatted with her hand outstretched, a baby on her lap. Around a corner, three children watched a man skin a goat; the blood ran down the gutter. In a marvelous landscape of geometric brick vats, enveloped in a horrible stench, men dipped skins into bright dyes.

At noon, the light and the heat were intense. I returned to my hotel and sank gratefully into the cool water of the pool.

The hotel was air conditioned. It had large public rooms paved in white terrazzo and marble, and several restaurants. Sliding glass doors opened onto the terrace and pool. There were comfortable, heavily upholstered seats, bright carpets, and everything was very clean. A small army of people wiped, cleared, polished, tended, and waited. A glass-enclosed elevator went to the upper floors. My room was light and spacious and it had a balcony. It also had a bathroom, a telephone, a radio, and a television set. Everything looked new. On the wall above the bed, in a gilt bamboo frame that matched the furniture, there was a photograph of the old medina.

As I waited out the heat of the day in my hotel room, it occurred to me that I had shot four rolls of film in the medina that morning, but I had not taken a single picture in the hotel.

TWO VERY DIFFERENT ENVIRONMENTS

The medina was a tourist's dream. Strange sights, smells, sounds, and tastes combined to intensify the sense of being a traveller in a strange place, among strange people, eating different food, and doing out-of-the-ordinary things. This

1   Fez, Morocco

In the Leather Quarter, brick vats filled with colored dyes create an environment that is almost natural in its directness and geometry; it is an environment that is delightful to look at but extremely unpleasant to work in. Photograph by the author.

was quite unlike anything at home. But the medina was more than exotic. It was also a rich sensuous experience: a place of exciting spatial sequences and dramatic contrasts, a juxtaposition of forms and functions that elicited deep-felt responses. It was a textbook of townscape design. Both as a visitor and as a designer, I found the medina fascinating and exciting.

I was somewhat less excited at the thought of living in the medina; it was too crowded, too dense, too dirty, too poor. The street system was totally confusing (without a guide I would have been hopelessly lost), but even more disorienting was the fact that the buildings, materials, food, wares, clothes, language, gestures, and activities, and the manner in which they presented themselves, were all so foreign to my experience that I had to accept what I saw at face value and could derive little social information from it. I could admire the architecture but I could not be sure about what went on there (was it an active mosque or a museum; was it public or private?), or about the conditions that were established for its use (was there an entrance fee, could I take photographs, was I properly clothed, was it proper for me as a stranger to accost a veiled woman?). The fact that I could not penetrate the surface appearance of things made it easier for me to see the medina as a succession of shapes and forms. My design training took over, and I looked with the "innocent eye" of the artist.

Unlike the medina, the hotel *was* a satisfying place to live and I felt I could operate there with complete competence. I could find my bearings with very little effort. I knew the way to my room. I could find a bathroom. I understood the difference between the restaurant and the coffee bar, and the items on the menu were familiar to me. Expensive materials, generous allocation of space, a high standard of care and maintenance, ready personal attention—all of these spoke of status, exclusiveness, and privilege. I had no trouble distinguishing between guests and employees, and even the classes of employees were distinguished by their clothes, manners, and stations. In the hotel I felt safe, protected from irritations and distractions. I felt I was in a comfortable and convenient place. I thought about the kind of changes that would make the medina a more acceptable place for me to live, and realized that these same changes would make the place less exotic, less distinctive, a less interesting place to visit.

It is clear that I was alternating between two different viewpoints, and that each viewpoint suggested different criteria for assessing the environment. As a tourist I looked for interesting and unusual experiences and I found them in the medina; but as a resident I looked for familiar and comfortable settings, and I found the hotel far more satisfying than the medina. It is unlikely that natives of Fez see the hotel and the medina as I did. I expect that the street pattern of the medina is more comprehensible to them than it was to me because they know more about the place and about the local culture,[1] so that the medina looks familiar and welcoming and good to come home to, while the hotel appears exotic and delightful and a desirable spot for a vacation. But I looked at Fez as a tourist, and as a tourist the hotel was no more than a base camp for forays into the medina. It was only when I thought of myself as a resident (and under the circumstances I downplayed the importance of this role) that I saw the hotel as the more attractive place. In looking at each place from two different viewpoints, I believe that I was experiencing a fundamental difference between residents and tourists (one could say residents and outsiders because tourists are, after all, the ultimate outsiders): each group sees the physical environment somewhat differently. This helps to explain why places that satisfy one group do not necessarily satisfy the other.

Obviously, the differences between Disneyworld and Monte Vista Terrace are not all in the eyes of the beholder, but nor are they all an expression of different functional requirements. I am suggesting that residents and outsiders not only have a different relationship with their physical environment, but (and this is clearly related) they perceive it in distinctly different ways.

Donald Appleyard (1976), in an insightful study of the residents of Ciudad Gyuana, a new city in Venezuela, identified three common modes of perception: the responsive, the operational, and the inferential (pp. 205–6). In the *responsive mode*, people perceived the city as a sensory experience. They saw trees, lights, sky, billboards, and buildings as colors, textures, sounds, smells, and tactile and kinesthetic experiences. In the *operational mode*, people perceived the city as a setting for personal actions and behavior. They paid particular attention to elements and qualities that were essential to the completion of regular tasks, trips, or operations. In the *inferential mode*, people perceived the city as a medium of communication. They were sensitive to the symbolic qualities of elements, matching experience against expectations and inferring beyond the information given.

Appleyard found that people were not locked into a single mode, but that they shifted between one mode and another. My experience in Fez suggests, however, that in particular circumstances (being a resident or an outsider, for example), one mode of perception predominates over the others.

Imagine that you are trying to find your way through strange surroundings, and you will find that the operational mode of perception predominates. When Hansel and Gretel were lost in the forest and they urgently needed to find their way out, they must have looked to the environment for clues that would point them in the direction of home. This is not to say that they did not admire the colors of the wildflowers, or recognize and avoid the poison ivy, but these things would have been of secondary interest and, from their perspective, less important than a trail of breadcrumbs. In the same way, I suggest, residents looking at their own home environments are especially sensitive to the social implications of what they see, and they favor the inferential mode of perception. Each mode of perception directs our attention to particular features of the environment, influences the way we define design problems, directs the search for solutions, and develops its own design theories and approaches.

THE RESPONSIVE MODE

When viewed in the responsive mode, design is concerned with qualities of the physical environment that evoke universal emotional responses. A good design is beautiful, a work of art. Books that deal with design in the responsive mode tend to be exemplars, source books of highly evocative physical settings. These settings are shown in photographs and drawings. The pictures are the primary source of information, and looking at them the reader captures something of the feeling of the original. The text directs the reader's attention, interprets, provides verbal labels, and points out the physical properties that have the power of arousal. Together, the pictures and text provide a lexicon of responses to design; they increase our awareness of the emotional possibilities of the physical environment. For example, in his description of a walk through Westminster, Cullen (1961) points out:

the shifting interplay of towers, spires and masts, all the intricacy of fresh alignments and groupings, the shafts of penetration and the sudden bunching of emphatic verticals into a dramatic knot, these are the rewards of the moving eye, but an eye which is open and not lazy. (p. 19)

Cullen points to features of the environment that can be enjoyed by all, irrespective of immediate purposes or cultural background, if they only know how to look.

Seen from the viewpoint of the responsive mode, the purpose of design theory is to describe general laws that will enable us to evoke strong emotional responses; for example, the feeling of being enclosed, excited, enticed, relaxed, exposed, assured, or removed; the feeling that one is outside looking in, or inside looking out. The usual approach of design theorists is to identify particularly evocative environments and, by studying their physical characteristics, to discover the properties that trigger emotional responses. Objects in the environment are seen mainly as abstractions (the play of masses and colors in space, brought together in light), or they are seen as archetypes (that is, as houses, fences, squares, statues, and buildings rather than as havens, barriers, familiar settings, memorials, and unsuitable neighborhoods), and the salient characteristics include harmony, balance, rhythm, good proportions, geometric form, and order. The responsive mode predisposes one to see the environment as a stimulus for the kinds of feelings and free associations contained in Francis Violich's sensitive description of a coastal town of Dalmatia (1983):

Pucisce rises on the steep slopes of a deep, watery cleavage—or fjord—on the north coast of Brac facing the mainland. The ultra blue inlet almost zig-zags its path to the townsite, obliterating fully any view or even any sense of connection with the sea. Pucisce looks inward completely on itself from its steep slopes, and as a visitor you feel yourself an intruder in a private world. Visible to all from the balconied dwellings, the newcomer feels conspicuous and foreign in a vast urban arena. The houses on the steep slopes appear to be seats on steep balconies with the thousand square "eyes" of the windows watching your every move seeking to know every newcomer whether resident or visitor. (p. 8)

The responsive mode makes extensive use of metaphors: places are described in terms of situations that evoke similar emotions. Take, for example, the following description of Edgartown, on Martha's Vineyard.

Edgartown . . . preserves the decorum of a black-tie dinner, where everyone manages to look his best while dressing very much like everyone else. Certain limited extravagances are allowed, like frills on a shirt or even a madras cummerbund, but there is a large area of agreement about forms, encouraged by an active and continuing tradition. There is pretty substantial agreement, too, about what cannot be included: no bare feet or even clip-on ties or their residential equivalent: shutters nailed to the wall. (Moore, Allen, and Lyndon, 1974, p. 5)

The responsive mode relies on observers' sensitivity to first impressions and not on their familiarity with a particular place, nor their knowledge of its origins or social significance, and consequently it is the predominant mode of the outsider. Le Corbusier (n.d.) refers to a sounding-board deep within each one of us that resonates to the universal qualities of good design. He defines the designer's task as one of arranging pure forms in such a way

THAT THE SIGHT OF THEM AFFECTS US IMMEDIATELY by their delicacy or vitality, their riot or their serenity, their indifference or their interest. (p. 16; caps in original)

Design in the responsive mode emerged from the field of art and aesthetics; it has a long history and has produced well integrated and time-tested principles. Design applications of the other two modes are quite recent; they rely extensively on findings in non-design fields like psychology, anthropology, and semiotics, and the design principles that have been produced are less comprehensive and less widely practiced by designers.

THE OPERATIONAL MODE

When observing in the operational mode, one's perceptions are guided by practical necessity: one looks to the environment for task-directed information. This is the predominant mode of the newcomer and the way-seeker, and the things one notices are quite different from those noticed by Violich or Moore. Here, for example, is a Jersey City resident's description of his environment in response to a request for directions (Lynch, 1960):

After you cross the highway, there's a going-up bridge; and after you come under the bridge, the first street you get to, there's a tannery packing company; the second corner after going on the avenue, you see banks on each side; and you come to the next corner, there's a radio store and a hardware store right close together on your right. On your left, before you cross the street, is a grocery store and a cleaner. You come up to 7th Street, and on 7th Street is a saloon facing you on the lefthand corner, and a vegetable market on the righthand—a liquor store on the right side of the road, on the left is a grocery store. The next street is 6th Street; there's no landmark except that you come under the railroad again. (p. 30)

A passage from Mark Twain's *Life on the Mississippi* (1929, pp. 79–80) illustrates the difference between the responsive and the operational modes. First, Twain described the river in the responsive mode—as it appeared to him when he saw it for the first time:

I still kept in mind a certain wonderful sunset which I witnessed when steamboating was new to me. A broad expanse of river was turned to blood; in the middle distance the red hue brightened into gold, through which a solitary log came floating, black and conspicuous; in one place a long slanting mark lay sparkling upon the water; in another the surface was broken by boiling, tumbling rings that were as many-tinted as an opal; where the ruddy flush was faintest, was a smooth spot that was covered with graceful circles and radiating lines, ever so delicately traced; the shore on our left was densely wooded, and the somber shadow that fell from this forest was broken in one place by a long, ruffled trail that shone like silver; and high above the forest wall a clean-stemmed dead tree waved a single leafy bough that glowed like a flame in the unobstructed splendor that was flowing from the sun. There were graceful curves, reflected images, woody heights, soft distances; and over the whole scene, far and near, the dissolving lights drifted steadily, enriching it every passing moment with new marvels of coloring.

Then Twain switched to the operational mode as he described the way the same scene appeared to him some years later, when he was an experienced riverboat pilot.

This sun means that we are going to have wind tomorrow; that floating log means that the river is rising, small thanks to it; that slanting mark on the water refers to a bluff reef which is going to kill somebody's steamboat one of these nights, if it keeps on stretching out like that; those tumbling 'boils' show a dissolving bar and a changing channel over there; the lines and circles in the slick water over yonder are a warning that that troublesome place is shoaling up dangerously; that silver streak in the shadow of the forest is the 'break' from a new snag, and he has located himself in the very best place he could have found to fish for steamboats; that tall dead tree, with a single living branch, is not going to last long, and then how is a body ever going to get through this blind place at night without the friendly old landmark?

Comparing his later perceptions with his earlier ones, Twain noted that

. . . the romance and beauty were all gone from the river. All the value any feature of it had for me now was the amount of usefulness it could furnish toward compassing the safe piloting of a steamboat.

This does not mean that the operational mode is incapable of producing pleasure (because when environmental information is clear and legible, the result can be pleasurable) but that the drive is for useful information rather than for sensory delight.

When viewed in the operational mode, design is concerned with features of the physical environment that affect the user's ability to execute necessary tasks. The purpose of design theory is to explain how people's use or nonuse or attitude toward the environment is affected by different physical forms and their order of presentation. Behavior and attitude are affected less directly by objective reality than by the perception of reality, and so one must look not only at the physical environment but also at people's mental images. Then, by comparing the physical and perceptual dimensions of the same place, we can identify physical qualities that are associated with, for example, recognition, orientation, and wayfaring.

Mental images serve as working maps of environmental information. To create these images, people select, arrange, relate, and often distort the physical features that they observe. They use the image to establish their location in relation to potential destinations and points of interest. A good design is thoroughly comprehensible to the user and facilitates effective action. Design theories in the operational mode tend to describe the physical environment in terms of the qualities of the perception; for example, as rich, distinctive, differentiated, structured, vivid, clear, articulated, or developing.

THE INFERENTIAL MODE

The inferential mode, like the operational mode, directs one's attention to environmental information, but this time it is information that reveals one's authority and social position relative to other users.[2] The inferential mode focuses on symbolic elements, whose meanings are often unintentional and whose significance varies with their social context. Meaning colors the appearance of objects, so that an object actually looks different if it assumes new significance. This is illustrated in the following passage by William James, taken from *On a Certain Blindness in Human Beings* (quoted by David Lowenthal, 1968):

Journeying in the mountains of North Carolina, I passed by a large number of "coves" . . . which had been newly cleared and planted. The impression on my mind was one of unmitigated squalor. The settler had . . . cut down the more manageable trees, and left their charred stumps. . . . The larger trees he had girdled and killed . . . and had set up a tall zigzag rail fence around the scene of his havoc. . . . Finally, he had irregularly planted the intervals between the stumps and trees with Indian corn. . . . The forest had been destroyed; and what has "improved" it out of existence was hideous, a sort of ulcer, without a single element of artificial grace to make up for the loss of Nature's beauty.

Then a mountaineer told James, "Why, we ain't happy here, unless we are getting one of these coves under cultivation."

I instantly felt that I had been losing the whole inward significance of the situation. . . . To me the clearings (were) . . . naught but . . . a mere ugly picture on the retina. . . . But when *they* looked on the hideous stumps, what they thought of was personal victory. The chips, the girdled trees, and the vile split rails spoke of honest sweat, persistent toil and final reward.

When viewed in the inferential mode, design is concerned with features of the physical environment that carry social messages, and a good design is one that clarifies, supports, and confirms social relationships.

From this viewpoint, the purpose of design theory is to identify physical features of the environment that carry social messages, and explain the ways in which these messages can affect social attitudes and behavior. Objects in the environment are seen in terms of the information that they convey; they represent records of events, achievements, and aspirations; they are indicators of social class, status, role, and affiliation; and cues to ownership and use of property. Objects are referred to as messages, symbols, signs, or markers; while the environment might be described as appropriated, controlled, personalized, safe, cared for, private, threatening, or friendly. Because meanings are acquired over a period of time and through the process of use and association, people respond not only to how the environment looks, but also to how it got to look that way.

When designers look at the environment in the inferential mode, they do not see impersonal spaces, but settings for behavior. Design is a visual language, and we must choose the medium, the elements, and the tone that best convey a desired message. We are, therefore, sensitive not only to the intrinsic qualities of objects, but to the associations that they have for those who will use them; and we recognize that the significance of objects (as of words) and their power to affect behavior depend to a large extent on context.

To summarize, I have tried to show that both the way we see our environment and the way that we evaluate it are influenced by our mode of perception. In the responsive mode we look for delight; in the operational, understanding; and in the inferential mode, meaning. An ideal environment will achieve high scores on all modes; but under certain circumstances we value one mode more than another, and high ratings on a more valued mode can compensate for low ratings on a less valued mode. Each mode of perception has its own theories about what makes good design. If we want to understand design, we must recognize the validity of different points of view.

NOTES

1. According to Geertz et al. (1979), there are special image elements that help people move around a traditional Islamic city. These include *derbs*—small streets of neighbors, each bearing the name of a particular family, and quarters—sections of the city, each of which is perceived as a separate district even though it is not defined by clear boundaries.

2. In the inferential mode we are also aware of the historical and stylistic associations of visual motifs. Such meanings are useful for purposes of identification, but when it comes to influencing behavior they are less important to residents than they are to outsiders, and they are less important than meanings that derive from use and personal experience.

2

Believing Is Seeing

Residents and outsiders look at the environment in different ways, and they
see different things.

Osbert Sitwell (1933) has a story about a group of people who went up Mount
Sinai for a picnic. They are the usual cast of characters that novelists bring
together in doomed hotels and in planes with engine trouble. When they
reached the top of the mountain, they were enveloped in a strange cloud. There
was a roaring wind, lightning, thunder, and the sound of trumpets, bells, and
gongs. Then there was a flash, and two stone tablets of the Law fell to the
ground.

One by one the picnickers went to inspect the tablets.

The palaeontologist was so taken with the composition of the stone he never
noticed that there was an inscription, and the artist noticed the inscription but
was so taken with the beauty of the calligraphy that he never read it; but each of
the other members of the party managed to read at least a sentence or two. The
male chauvinist read, "Honor thy Father, who embodies the principal of the
Dominant Male . . . "; the gossip columnist read, "Thou shalt bear false witness
against thy neighbor"; the industrialist read, "Thou shalt not buy foreign
goods"; the soldier read, "Thou shalt do no murder, except when dressed in
uniform issued under the War Office Regulations"; the soldier's wife, who took
both sides on every issue, read, "Thou shalt not kill the beasts of the field,
except for eating or for sport"; and the bishop, with a genius for embracing
popular causes, read, "Safety first." The Arab chieftain read, "There is no God

but Allah," and so he ordered his tribesmen to capture the party; they killed the men, and imprisoned the women.

This story satirizes the fact that we all see what we look for; that if we change what we know or believe about an object, we effectively change its appearance. If you doubt that this is true, then take an object, tell a group of people what it is, and ask them what they think of its appearance. Then tell them it is really something else and ask them what they think of its appearance now. You will see their evaluations change.

Say, for example, you show them the object pictured in photo 2. Tell them that the object is a celebrated ritual figure from a little-known African tribe, believed to house ancestral spirits and to possess great power, and they will look at the object as a *medium*, where every feature is charged with meaning: circles signify continuity of time, grasses represent man's link with nature, dark colors are threatening, braiding implies that lives are intertwined, and so on.

Tell them that the object is called "Texture Study" and is by a young San Francisco artist, and they will look at the object as a *masterpiece*, focusing on its formal qualities and on the skill and originality of the artist: is it well proportioned, balanced and harmonious; does it express the nature of the materials; is it original and well crafted?

Tell them that the object was bought as a birthday present for a three-year-old child, and they will look at it as a *toy*, something that is amusing to look at and fun to play with: does it make a sound when you shake it, does anything happen when you turn it upside down, do the rings come off, does it stimulate the imagination?

Tell them that it is one of a new line of Magi-care industrial strength decorator air fresheners available at most supermarkets, and they will look at it as a *tool*, something that is essentially practical: is the decoration necessary, how much freshener does it hold, how much does it cost, can it be refilled, will it collect dust, is it awkward to use?

The object shown in the picture is "really" an African doll. I have found that people rate its appearance very differently if they have been told different things about it. They tend to give it high ratings as a *medium* (it is strange and mysterious) and as a *masterpiece* (it has a simple form and nice textures), a somewhat lower rating as a *toy* (one can't do much with it), and a low rating as a *tool* (it is quite impractical). Its appearance effectively changes even though the physical elements—the composition of the object, the light, and the observers—remain constant.[1]

What we know or believe about an object, then, affects the way it looks.[2] What we see in a painting is influenced by our knowledge of art history and theory.[3] An original painting looks different from an identical copy because we know that it is "the real thing" and this adds something special to its appearance: the copy may capture the painting's objective appearance but it can-

2   Artifact

Is this object well designed? Before you answer that question you must first decide what the object is. Photograph by Kate Brower.

not capture its meaning, and meaning has a strong influence on our perceptions.[4] A small irregularity in the pattern of a handwoven rug shows the imprint of the weaver and makes the rug look more personal, but a similar irregularity in a machine woven rug implies poor quality control and makes the rug look flawed. Japanese restaurants display startlingly realistic reproductions of food items to depict their bill of fare, but the same objects in the museum gift shop demonstrate the artists' skill, and we buy them in order to impress our friends. An urbanite sees a field as a peaceful and natural landscape, where a farmer sees imposed order and the application of progressive farming principles (Nassauer and Westmacott, 1985). New information may change old perceptions: a string of beads bought as a fashion accessory is recognized to be a rosary, a worn decoy duck is rescued from the junkpile and displayed as an antique. Thompson (1979) writes about whole sections of London once seen as rat-infested slums, but now seen as historic treasures.

What we know affects not only how we see things, but also what we look at. When presented with a great deal of information—as in the case of an urban environment, for example—we must choose what objects to look at or we would be overwhelmed. Like Lorelei Lee in Paris (Loos, 1963), we focus our attention on objects that interest us and ignore the rest.[5]

[W]hen Dorothy and I went on a walk, we only walked a few blocks, but in a few blocks we read all of the famous historical names, like Coty and Cartier and I knew we were seeing something educational at last. . . . So when we stood at a place called the Place Vendome, if you turn your back on a monument they have in the middle and look up, you can see none other than Coty's sign. (p. 78)

Perception, then, is a creative not a mechanical act: we see what we look for and we look for things that interest us. Our perceptions are not mirror-images but interpretations of what is "out there," and it is these interpretations of the environment rather than its objective qualities that explain our attitudes and behaviors.[6] If our information and interests change, we see the same environment somewhat differently. This explains how it is possible for residents and outsiders to look at the same environment, and yet see it differently.

Perhaps the best way to introduce a discussion of differences in perception between residents and outsiders is to note that when an outsider changes into a resident the environment "looks" different. Herb Gans (1962) comments on such an experience in the West End of Boston.

My first visit to the West End left me with the impression that I was in Europe. Its high buildings set on narrow, irregularly curving streets, its Italian and Jewish restaurants and food stores, and the variety of people who crowded the streets when the weather was good—all gave the area a foreign and exotic flavor. . . . [L]ooking at the area as a tourist, I noted the highly visible and divergent characteristics that set it off from others with which I was familiar. And while the exotic quality of the West End did excite me, the dilapidation and garbage were depressing . . .

After a few weeks of living in the West End, my observations—and my perception of the area—changed drastically. . . . [I]n wandering through the West End, and using it as a resident, I developed a kind of selective perception, in which my eye focused only on those parts of the area that were actually being used by people. The dirt and spilled-over garbage . . . were not as noticeable as during my initial observations. . . . The exotic quality of the stores and the residents also wore off as I became used to seeing them. (pp. 11–12)

Gans contrasts his perceptions as a resident with those of the ultimate outsider—a tourist.

There are different types of tourists, but one feature that is central to the tourist experience is that of being away from home, removed from the familiar scenes and activities of the workaday environment, and cut off from the ties, commitments, and responsibilities that dominate it.[7] Tourists do not have an enduring relationship with the visited environment and they do not feel responsible for what happens there. They are essentially observers rather than participants. What they know is based on first impressions, comparisons with other places, and images created by postcards, travel brochures, posters, signs, slide shows, and the like so that, to a large extent, they see what they previously knew to be there. Tourists depend heavily on the physical environment as a source of information on their whereabouts, and they feel most comfortable in places where the features are distinctive and the orientational information is clear and vivid; that is, where there is a strong "sense of place." In order to intensify the feeling of being away from it all, tourists look for experiences that are new and different from those at home.

The residential experience is quite different.[8] For most residents, their home environment is the most personal of places, the setting for intimate and enduring relationships, a refuge from the world, a confirmation of self, a locus of community, and a symbol of continuity. It represents an investment, and a long-term commitment, a place where one comes to recover from one's wounds and rekindle one's energies.[9] Residents look to the residential area for shelter, security, comfort, convenience, control, cleanliness, and respectability, not for adventure; and the novel, exciting, interesting places that attract tourists are often seen as undesirable to live in. In the same way, a place that looks attractive to live in does not necessarily look attractive to a visitor.

Residents acquire information about their residential area over an extended period of time. In the course of repeated interactions with the same people, buildings, facilities, and activities, features of the environment become embedded in the subconsciousness, so that residents no longer seem to be aware of them: they know they are there but they only notice them when they are changed or removed. Think, for example, of the experience of driving down a familiar road:

Familiarity with a route will cause marked differences in perception and attitude. The first time traveller, predicting only with those cues he can glean from the landscape, will be highly attentive to any information relevant to his goal. . . . [T]he commuter, on the other hand, sure of his prediction, may absorb all necessary information subliminally. His active interest is aroused only by unexpected traffic movements or new changes in the environment. (Appleyard 1965, p. 183)

Or think of one's responses to everyday objects around the house:

It gets to be that I become so familiar with what's on the walls, that I don't know it's there and I don't even have to see it. I *know* it's there. If you were to take it down and remove it, I would know it's gone immediately. If anything's out of place, I would know that it's out of place. (Csikszentmihalyi and Rochberg-Halton, 1981, p. 183)

At the same time that they seem oblivious to things that outsiders find quite striking, residents notice things that escape the attention of outsiders, and they see things in the environment that do not exist for outsiders. Residents' interactions with the environment represent personal and collective struggles, accomplishments, responsibilities, and changes, and these become associated with the physical settings in which they occur and charge them with purely local meanings. These meanings can be so powerful as to supersede physical qualities as the dominant influence on perception; that is, residents see a place as home, birthplace, or investment, before they see it as a physical form.[10] This is apparent when residents talk about their home environment. Here, for example (Brower, 1985), one resident talks about the sculpture of a nude woman in the park in front of his house, while another describes a local restaurant.

[I] walk by there every day. . . . [A] tourist would see that . . . and say, "Oh, that's beautiful." But when I'm on my way to Peabody [Conservatory of Music] in the middle of the afternoon on a weekday, sometimes I think maybe I shouldn't be looking at this sensuous woman in the middle of the day like this . . . so sometimes as I walk by it I look the other way because I don't think I should be looking at it. But if you're a tourist, you don't go through that. You think it's all right.

J——'s Restaurant . . . has the best coffee because one of his old socks is in the pot. I don't know if that's true or not, but that's the rumor around the neighborhood. Wonderful coffee.

Local meanings can be positive, enhancing the residents' view of the physical environment, or they can be negative, making an otherwise innocuous environment look depressing, scary, or unpleasant; but positive or negative, these meanings represent emotional linkages between objects and observers that residents feel and outsiders do not. Unless we actively dislike an environment, it will become more reassuring, restful, and secure as we become more familiar with it. This may be because familiar environments confirm who we are and affirm what we stand for; or it may be because we feel more competent there— we know what there is and where to find it and so we are able to pay more attention to the job at hand; or it may be that familiarity operates independently of meaning and that repeated exposure, by itself, is sufficient to give us a more positive attitude toward our environment.[11] Whatever the reason, what is important here is that familiar environments seem safer and more satisfying than unfamiliar ones. No matter what the objective circumstances, when asked to rate different residential environments people tend to rate familiar ones higher than unfamiliar ones, and residents rate their own environments higher than outside observers.[12]

The fact that residents prefer familiar environments does not mean that they want everything about them to be equally familiar. The effect of too much familiarity is told in Alan Jay Lerner's lyrics for the musical, *Gigi.*

Don't you marvel at the power of the mighty Eiffel tower
Knowing there it will remain evermore?
Climbing up to the sky, over ninety stories high . . .
How many stories?
Ninety!
How many yesterday?
Ninety!
And tomorrow?
Ninety!
It's a bore.

There are several strategies we resort to in order to prevent our home environment from becoming overly familiar. Perhaps the most common strategy is to modify (but not substantially change) the familiar image of the place. This can be done by rearranging the furniture, buying new drapes, moving the pictures around, or trying a new color on the walls (Kron, 1983). Another strategy is to get away for a while: when we return there is a period during which we see things afresh. There is, of course, always the danger that we will notice flaws and inadequacies that familiarity had blinded us to. This is what happened to Mole in Kenneth Grahame's (1961) *The Wind in the Willows.* Mole, who had been staying with his friend Rat, had an irresistible urge to return home. His first impression, when he eventually got there, was disappointing:

[He] saw the cheerless, deserted look of the long-neglected house, and its narrow, meager dimensions, its worn and shabby contents—and collapsed again in a hall-chair, his nose in his paws. 'O Ratty!' he cried dismally, 'Why did I ever do it? Why did I bring you to this poor, cold little place . . . '(p. 87)

But the period of fresh perception was a brief one, and features soon faded once again into the general atmosphere. By the time Mole went to bed, the familiar pattern had re-established itself, and

. . . ere he closed his eyes, he let them wander around his old room, mellow in the glow of the firelight that played or rested on familiar and friendly things which had long been unconsciously a part of him, and now smilingly received him back without rancour. . . . [I]t was good to think that he had this to come back to, this place which was all his own, these things which were so glad to see him again and could always be counted upon for the same simple welcome. (p. 96)

Another strategy for restoring jaded perceptions is to look at the familiar environment as if through the eyes of a stranger. This is a common empathetic response to the presence of outsiders, because residents want their home environment to look good to their guests and they are upset if it does not.

This is really one of the most pitiful things about Jersey City. There isn't anything that if someone came here from a far place, that I could say, "Oh, I want you to see this . . . " (Lynch, 1960, p. 29)

For residents to look at their home from the visitors' viewpoint does not require special talent (although some people are better at it than others), but it comes more easily in those parts of the environment that are meant to be used by outsiders, like streets, entrances, and living rooms, than in "backstage" spaces like bedrooms, basements, and attics.[13] The view as it is seen through "strange eyes" is especially important to residents who are sensitive to "appearances" (which is to say the way things appear to outsiders) and who see the home environment as a public expression of self.

Just as residents are bored in home environments where everything is totally familiar, so outsiders are uncomfortable in environments where everything is totally unfamiliar—they feel out of place, out of control, lost. Some people like to feel at home wherever they are.

So Dorothy and I came to the Ritz [in London] and it is delightfully full of Americans. I mean you would really think it was New York because I always think that the most delightful thing about travelling is to always be running into Americans and to always feel at home. (Loos, 1963, p. 57)

In order to make outsiders feel more at home, many places offer lodgings that incorporate the features and values of the visitors' home environment; and they offer travel agencies, group tours, guides, reception centers, and specially staged events to provide outsiders with information, interpretation, and assistance.[14] There are those, however, who believe that the resident experience is the only true experience of a place, and that these institutions dupe the visitors by insulating them from the residents, and place them in an environment that is no more than a mirage, something that has been artifically created.[15]

In the same way that residents sometimes look at a familiar environment through the eyes of an outsider, so outsiders sometimes override their automatic perceptions and look at a strange environment from a resident's viewpoint (Brower, 1985). Usually, there is little inducement for outsiders to do this, and it requires a conscious effort; but it explains how professional designers, who seldom have any experience of living in the environments they create, are able to act on behalf of prospective residents. (Of course, designers must also be prepared to play to the residents rather than to outsiders like the general public and other designers.)

The fact that residents and outsiders both recognize the validity of the other viewpoint means that if a place can incorporate elements both of continuity and of change, it can be attractive both as a place to live and as a place to visit. Some places achieve this through forms that are so insistent, and images that are so evocative, that one does not tire of them. Others create the effect of variety even though they may change very little, because as soon as we become familiar with them at one level, another level opens up for exploration. Complex environments that offer the opportunity for continuity at one level and change at another have the best potential for satisfying the need of both residents and outsiders.

NOTES

1. In "Tools, toys, masterpieces, mediums" (1975) I suggested these four ways of looking at objects.

2. Gregory (1968) describes the process of perception as follows:

Visual perception involves "reading" from retinal images a host of characteristics of objects that are not represented directly by the images in the eyes. The image does not convey directly many important characteristics of objects; whether they are hard or soft, heavy or light, hot or cold. Nonvisual characteristics must somehow be associated with the visual image by individual learning . . . for objects to be recognised from their images. Such learning is essential for perception; without it one would have mere stimulus-response behavior.

Perception seems to be a matter of looking up information that has been stored about objects and how they behave in various situations. The retinal image does little more than select the relevant stored data, . . . behavior is determined by the contents of the entry rather than by the stimulus that provoked the search.

For further information about the perceptual process see Gregory, 1970; S. Kaplan and R. Kaplan, 1982.

3. In *The Painted Word* (1975), Tom Wolfe discusses the way that art critics have shaped the popular perception of Modern Art:

Not "seeing is believing", you ninny, but "believing is seeing" for Modern Art has become completely literary: the paintings and other works exist only to illustrate the text. (p. 7)

4. Horace Rumpole, defending an artist who is charged with forging a painting, questions whether the painting in question is admired because it is beautiful or because it is the work of a particular painter (Mortimer, 1984, p. 34).

'Mrs. De Moyne. Wouldn't you agree,' I asked as I rose to cross-examine, 'that you bought a very beautiful picture?'

'Yes,' Mrs. De Moyne admitted.

'So beautiful you were prepared to pay sixty thousand pounds for it?'

'Yes, I was.'

'And is it still the same beautiful picture? The picture hasn't changed since you bought it, has it, Mrs. De Moyne? Not by one drop of paint! Is the truth of the matter that you are not interested in art but merely in collecting autographs!'

For a discussion about what we see when we look at paintings, and about the difference between looking at an original and a reproduction, see John Berger (1977, pp. 7–33).

5. William James (1950) expressed it as follows:

Millions of items in the outward order are present to my senses which never properly enter into my experience. Why? Because they have no *interest* for me. *My experience is what I attend to.* Only those items which I *notice* shape my mind—without selective interest, experience is an utter chaos. (p. 402)

Milgrim (1970) identified selective perception as a mechanism for coping with information overload.

6. Koffka (1935) distinguished between the objective or "geographical environment" and the perceived or "behavioral environment"; and Chein (1954) explained it this way:

The [geographical environment] refers to the objective physical and social environment in which the individual is immersed. The [behavioral environment] refers to the environment as it is perceived and reacted to by the behaving individual: it may bear little resemblance to the geographical environment, being an organized "interpretation" of the latter based on recollections, anticipations, perceptual distortions and omissions, and upon reasonably correct perceptions. The behavioral environment deletes from and alters, as well as adds to the geographic environment.

7. Smith (1977) defines a tourist as "a temporarily leisured person who voluntarily visits a place away from home for the purpose of experiencing a change." (p. 2) For classifications of different types of tourists see also U.S. Department of Commerce, 1981; Pearce, 1982. For discussions of the tourist experience see Appleyard, 1976 and 1979a; MacCannell, 1973 and 1976; Pearce, 1982; Bosselman, 1978; and Smith, 1977.

8. For discussions of the resident experience see Fried, 1982; Csikszentmihalyi and Rochberg-Halton, 1981; Lynch, 1981; Steele, 1981; Winkel, 1981; Appleyard, 1976 and 1979b; Becker, 1978; Birch et al., 1977; Rapoport, 1977; Lofland, 1973; and Lansing and Marans, 1969, p. 197.

9. Residents who perceive their home environment as threatening may not form all of these positive associations (see Rainwater, 1966), but this does not mean that these associations are inappropriate or undesirable.

10. Czikszentmihalyi and Rochberg-Halton (1981) did a study of objects in the home that are important to residents. They have the following things to say about meanings.

[T]he total context of artifacts in a household acts as a constant sign of familiarity, telling us who we and our kindred are, what we have done or plan to do, and in this way reduces the amount of information we have to pay attention to in order to act with ease. . . . One of the most important functions of household possessions, then, is to provide a *familiar* environment, which can reflect the order, control and significance of its inhabitants, and thus enable them to channel their psychic energy more effectively within it. (p. 185)

11. Zajonc (1968) cites an experiment where nonsense words were introduced to participants as "real" words in a foreign language. Some words were shown more frequently than others. When participants were then asked to guess the meanings of the words, the more frequently heard words were said to have more positive meanings. In another experiment, participants were shown photographs of strange men, some photographs being shown more frequently than others. When asked how they might like each of the men on the photographs, participants showed a marked preference for photographs that they had seen more frequently.

12. Palmer (1983) showed residents of Syracuse, New York, 28 pictures of the same

house, but each picture showed a different landscape treatment of the front yard. Participants were asked to indicate how much they would like their own front yard to look like each of those in the pictures, and they were asked to identify the picture that looked most like their front yard. The findings showed that participants preferred the front yards that were most like their own.

Michelson (1976, p. 91) in a study of residential preferences, found that people who lived further from their friends expressed a preference for lower density living, and that people who shopped outside their present neighborhood thought of an ideal neighborhood as one without commercial uses.

Warren (1982), in a national survey of neighborhoods, found that over half of the residents interviewed rated their neighborhood at seven or more on a ten point scale, and more than three quarters rated their neighborhood at five or more.

One could interpret these findings to mean that people liked their present environment because they had made a careful choice in the first place, and not because it had grown familiar to them. Such an interpretation was not possible in the following study. Rosen (1971) looked at the housing preferences of residents in two public housing buildings in Baltimore, where apartments were assigned on the basis of priority and availability rather than choice. Residents were asked to indicate how desirable it was for apartments to include certain design features, such as a balcony, a separate bedroom, a separate kitchen, and extra storage space. Some apartments already had one or more of these features while others did not. Rosen found in almost every case that participants expressed a preference for features already present in their apartment.

The sanguinary effect of familiarity also changes people's perception of danger. In an eight-city survey of crime and fear of crime in residential areas, Hinderlang, Gottfredson, and Garofalo (1978) found that residents felt the crime problem was less severe in their neighborhood than in other areas, regardless of the objective circumstances. Familiarity may not make a dangerous neighborhood seem safe, but it makes it seem safer than other, less familiar neighborhoods. These findings are supported by other studies; see Dubow, McCabe, and Kaplan, 1979, p. 9.

A number of studies have found that people who are familiar with an environment give it a higher rating than strangers do.

Keller (1968, p. 108) cites a study of housing areas in San Juan, Puerto Rico, where objective measures (developed and applied by outsiders) indicated that living conditions were shockingly inadequate. The study found, however, that residential satisfaction was high, 70 percent of the respondents rating their areas as good places to live.

Grigsby and Rosenburg (1975) in a study of housing in Baltimore, found that families tended to give their homes a higher rating than interviewers or housing inspectors. Even in the case of families who lived in seriously substandard housing (according to the city housing code), 50 percent were not dissatisfied with their accommodations (p. 74).

Campbell, Converse, and Rogers (1976) asked resident respondents and interviewers to describe their neighborhood using twelve dimensions. They found that residents viewed their neighborhood in more pleasant terms than interviewers (p. 243). They also found that poor respondents expressed almost as much overall satisfaction with their neighborhoods as wealthy respondents expressed with theirs (p. 480).

In a study of three areas in Ahmedabad, Desai (1980) obtained ratings of environmental quality from residents and from independent raters: in almost all cases, the residents' ratings were higher than those of the independent raters.

Lansing and Marans (1969) compared neighborhood ratings by planners and residents.

They found that 88 percent of the people living in neighborhoods judged unpleasant by the planner liked their neighborhood at least moderately well, while only 12 percent disliked it (p. 197).

Familiarity even affects the critical eye of the professional designer. Imamoglu (1979) asked architects to rate the quality of the living rooms in sixty housing units in Ankara, Turkey, and he compared their ratings with those of the householders themselves. He found that the householders rated the rooms more positively than the architects. Imamoglu then asked architects to evaluate living rooms belonging to *other architects.* He found that the architect-householders rated their rooms higher than the architect-evaluators.

13. Of course, newcomers behave in much the same way whether they are residents or outsiders: both move with increasing confidence as routes and landmarks become more familiar. Cooper (1981) in a study of visitors at a holiday resort, found that new arrivals tended to go first to the "center," where the physical environment gave the strongest and clearest informational signals; but gradually they ventured into other areas, first paying great attention to their surroundings, and then moving with increasing confidence as routes and landmarks became more familiar. Hudson (1975) found that new residents used facilities that were near home or their place of work. As time passed, their activities extended over a wider geographical area. Aldskogins (1977) came up with similar findings.

For further discussions about mental images—their structure, effect on behavior, and change over time—see Evans, Marrero, and Butler, 1981; Canter, 1977, pp. 67–69; Downs and Stea, 1977; Appleyard, 1976; Devlin, 1976; and Lynch, 1960, p. 49.

14. "I run my hotels the way I run my home," Leona M. Helmsley proclaims in an advertisement for Harley Hotels (*Ozark*, September 1985). "My home was not designed just to be beautiful. My first considerations are always comfort and convenience. And that's how I planned the rooms at every Harley Hotel."

15. Boorstin (1961) characterizes tourist environments as a cultural mirage, and events that are arranged especially for tourists as pseudo-events. He argues that in catering to tourists, host countries debase the local culture, noting that "earnest, honest natives embellish their ancient rites, change, enlarge and spectacularize their festivals, so that tourists will not be disappointed" (p. 103).

For further discussions about the superficiality of tourist environments see MacCannell, 1976; Dubos 1972, pp. 24–25; and Mitford, 1959.

3

Residents and Outsiders

Residents and outsiders have different priorities when they come to evaluate the environment, but their positions are not necessarily in opposition so it is possible for both groups to find satisfaction in the same environment.

I have argued that we do not see our home environment as outsiders do. The things we look for as residents do not necessarily impress us as visitors, just as the things that draw us to strange places do not necessarily make us want to live there. If we think of the ideal place to live, most people envision a place in the country or a quiet suburb, but some people who can afford the suburbs prefer to live in places that are more lively, distinctive, and socially diverse, with the kinds of streets, buildings, stores, bars, cafes, and institutions that invite non-residents in. Here, for example, residents talk about two in-town neighborhoods in Baltimore, known as Fells Point and Mount Vernon.

I was living north of Towson when we decided to move down here, and this is one of the things I really like: in the evening we sit out in our folding chairs and talk (with our neighbors). And we don't do that in Towson.

When I moved here my mother says, "Oh, now you finally have some place to go early in the morning," because living any place else, what else opens at five-thirty, six o'clock in the morning?

I'm a history nut. . . . That's one of the things that brings us down here.

[T]he biggest reason we moved in here was because of the view of the city from our windows. It's really nice at night, and we can see the fireworks whenever they have something going on.

If we say that the qualities that make an environment good for residents are different from those that make it good for outsiders, then how do we explain why people choose to live in areas that cater to outsiders? Are these atypical residents? Are their perceptions closer to those of outsiders than residents, and do they, therefore, choose to live in these areas because of their outsider-pleasing qualities? Or do they choose the areas in spite of these qualities, because the essential residential qualities of the suburbs are also found in Fells Point and Mount Vernon?

I looked to the literature for answers to these questions. From reports and papers about sources of satisfaction in residential areas[1] I learned that residents have a strong preference for places that are well maintained, socially desirable, and safe. They also prefer places that are good looking, provide adequate services, and are quiet and private. Preference for a natural setting and for variety were each mentioned in one study. Then I reviewed material that dealt with outsiders' environmental preferences.[2] I learned that outsiders have a strong preference for places that are unusual and interesting. They also prefer places that are central, recreational, good looking, and lively. Qualities mentioned in only one study were public use, adequate services, pedestrian access, and safety.

A comparison of residents' and outsiders' preferences suggests that they are different but, in the main, not mutually incompatible. A place can be central and also socially desirable, interesting and also well maintained, unusual and also safe, and such a place will go far toward satisfying both residents and outsiders. But a place cannot be quiet at the same time that it is lively, and it cannot be both private and public. If these qualities are important to each group, they could be the qualities that separate good resident-places from good outsider-places.

Further analysis based on the literature would, however, be of questionable validity because it means comparing different studies, using different methods and in the context of different environments, each study consisting of resident-only or outsider-only responses. And so, in order to identify the nature and importance of the criteria used by residents and outsiders, we conducted a study in the Fells Point and Mount Vernon areas in Baltimore—both residential neighborhoods that are well used by visitors.[3] A total of 103 residents of Fells Point and Mount Vernon were interviewed in the study. Some were asked about their own neighborhood and others were asked to respond as visitors in the other neighborhood. In addition, 22 out-of-towners, all unfamiliar with Fells Point and Mount Vernon, were interviewed. The purpose of the interviews was to identify and compare the criteria that residents and visitors used to evaluate the environment. Before discussing the main findings, however, we should know something about the two neighborhoods and about the people who participated in the study.

The following descriptions of the study areas are adapted from a visitor's guide to Baltimore (Citizen's Planning and Housing Association, 1976).

Fells Point. Fells Point was founded as a separate town in 1763, and the area

3   Fells Point

Modest buildings with apartments, stores, bars, and businesses line the waterfront along Thames Street, in Fells Point. Photograph by Kate Brower.

still retains its basic street layout and a large number of the buildings that were there before 1830. After a long and active history as a center, first for shipbuilding and then for industry, the area declined. In 1960 it was threatened by destruction to make way for an interstate expressway. A long fight not only saved the neighborhood from the highway, but it also sparked a surge of renewal and restoration. The population of Fells Point is diverse, to say the least, giving it a vitality unlike any other Baltimore neighborhood. It has something for everyone—the old Broadway Market, junk/antique shops, restaurants, bars, theaters, and galleries. The visual and activity focal point of the neighborhood is Market Square, where Broadway meets the water.

Mount Vernon. No neighborhood can make a stronger claim for being Baltimore's "heart of the city" community than Mount Vernon. Reminiscent of many of London's pedestrian-oriented in-city neighborhoods, Mount Vernon offers magnificent old brownstone townhouses interspersed with many of the city's most notable historic and cultural landmarks. The heart of Mount Vernon is Mount Vernon Place, a cross of green parks, fountains, and statues surrounding Baltimore's Washington Monument. Numerous boutiques, pubs, and restaurants round out Mount Vernon's offerings and make it one of the city's more diverse neighborhoods.

Analysis of U.S. census statistics showed that the composition of the people who lived in Fells Point and Mount Vernon was not that of a typical residential suburb: there were relatively fewer married couples, fewer households with young children, and a higher percentage of renters.[4] Mount Vernon was further from the suburban norm than Fells Point: this is evident both from the census figures, and from descriptive and demographic data collected in the study. Residents spoke of Fells Point as a residential community that was popular with visitors, but they spoke of Mount Vernon as downtown. This difference was evident in the way residents described places of interest in the two neighborhoods: in Fells Point they talked about their local significance, but in Mount Vernon they referred to their regional importance.

In Fells Point, they said:

That's J——'s. J——'s Restaurant. . . . [Y]ou can go down and have a cup of the best coffee from anywhere, and a doughnut, and pick up all the neighborhood information, and a lot of neighborhood people meet there. It's a real neighborhood spot.

That's where I buy all my chickens and eggs and stuff. They're very nice people to deal with, and a lot of people from here go there. . . .

I've been going to that church all my life. As far as I can remember.

In Mount Vernon, they said:

Mount Vernon has some of what I consider the finest restaurants on the East Coast.

It's the original [Washington] monument and I'm very proud of that fact and I tell everybody. . . .

4   Mount Vernon

Grand old houses—now apartments, clubs, schools, and professional offices—face the park in Mount Vernon Place. Photograph by Kate Brower.

Baltimore has more spires than Vatican City, according to a brochure I read before I moved here, and that's one of the most impressive spires in the city.

Participants living in Fells Point were more likely to have other relatives in the neighborhood (in percentages: Fells Point, 28; Mount Vernon, 8), to have friends there (Fells Point, 76; Mount Vernon, 60) and, in fact, to have most of their friends there (Fells Point, 72; Mount Vernon 32). Fells Pointers were more likely to do their banking, and shop for food and household supplies in the neighborhood, while Mount Vernon residents were more likely to patronize local restaurants, bars, and shows.

It seems, then, that while Fells Point and Mount Vernon were both in-town neighborhoods, Fells Point was perceived primarily as a residential community and Mount Vernon primarily as a place for tourists.

The method used to identify evaluative criteria was based on personal construct theory (Kelly, 1955; Harrison and Sarre, 1971). According to this theory, we assess an environment on a number of cognitive constructs. We can think of each construct as a rating scale that has at its ends the opposite extremes of a particular quality (like *varied* and *all the same*). In evaluating an environment, a person selects the relevant constructs, rates the environment on each construct, and then uses these ratings as the basis for an overall assessment. Using the methodology of personal construct theory, it is possible to identify both the constructs that people think are relevant to a particular place and their ratings on each construct.

The first step in the study was to obtain photographs of places that characterized each neighborhood.[5] We asked local residents to take pictures of objects and places in the neighborhood that were important to them; then we interviewed each participant-photographer and discussed the significance of each photograph. We took conducted tours arranged by local tour agencies in order to see what sights in each neighborhood were of interest to tourists, and we acquired picture postcards of Fells Point and Mount Vernon that were on sale in the city and photographed the views that sold best. Professional tour guides who were familiar with the neighborhoods were invited to select from these photographs the ones that they felt captured the "feel" of the area—that they might use to attract visitors. In this way we came up with the ten places that were most commonly associated with each neighborhood, and a set of photographs that showed what residents and outsiders saw as the most characteristic views of each place.

We selected a sample of residents and non-residents in each neighborhood.[6] We took non-residents on a tour of the places shown on the photographs, and then interviewed each participant using the photographs as stimuli. There were two rounds of interviews, each with a different subsample of residents and non-residents.

The first round of interviews involved 20 participants. The purpose of these interviews was to find out what bipolar constructs were used to evaluate the neighborhoods. Participants were shown the pictures three at a time (the composition of each triad was determined by random selection) and each time they were asked:

Tell me one quality that is especially important to a [visitor or resident] that you can see in two of the pictures but not in the third. How is the third picture different from the other two?

The response to this question took the form of a bipolar construct. The procedure was repeated with eight different triads, and so we elicited eight bipolar constructs from each participant. Some of the poles were expressed as single words (safe/unsafe) and others as descriptive phrases (would feel comfortable there/would not hang around there). After we had completed all the interviews we reviewed the content of each construct, grouped related constructs together, and gave each grouping a label that encapsulated the original words and phrases. In this way we arrived at twelve supraconstructs. They were:

Something interesting to see and do	—	Nothing interesting to see and do
Completed, finished	—	Changing, not completed
Good looking	—	Not good looking
Unusual, unique	—	Not unusual, commonplace
Variety, mix of interests and activities	—	Sameness, similar interests and activities
Quiet, peaceful	—	Busy, lively
Public, strangers welcome	—	Private, strangers not welcome
Many needs catered to	—	Few needs catered to
Safe at night	—	Not safe at night
Central, visible	—	Out-of-the-way, hidden
Cared for	—	Neglected
Good for walking	—	Not good for walking

These twelve constructs represented an inventory of the qualities that residents and outsiders took into account when assessing Fells Point and Mount Vernon. They were essentially the same qualities that showed up in the literature.

The second round of interviews was designed to identify which of the constructs were more important than others, and to whom. A total of 105 participants were involved. Participants were asked to rate each picture on each construct. (They were asked to rate each picture on a scale that ranged from *interesting* to *not interesting*, then again on a scale that ranged from *completed* to *changing*, and so on.) Then, when they had rated all of the pictures according to all of the constructs, they were asked to identify the positive pole of each construct and to rate its importance. There were, then, two sets of ratings: construct ratings for each place and importance ratings for each positive pole.

Looking at the construct ratings, we find some agreement in the way that residents and outsiders rated places. Commercial streets were generally seen as public places; stores were more public than parks, museums, and churches. Residential streets, by contrast, were private places, although it seems that when a residential street was well used by outsiders—a particularly quaint or historic street, for example—residents emphasized the *public* nature and outsiders the *private* nature of the street. Residential streets were also rated as the least varied of places, and commercial streets as the most varied.

We also found differences in the way residents and outsiders rated the same place. Outsiders were more likely to look for interesting and unusual features, and they were also more likely to find them: they scored places higher than residents did on both of these qualities. Places that were rated more interesting and unusual were also likely to be rated more good looking. Residents saw places in their own neighborhoods as less interesting, unusual, and good looking than outsiders did, and they saw them as less well cared for. In discussions, residents commented frequently and heatedly about litter and trash, and neglected pavements, buildings, and yards; and their ratings on the *cared for/neglected* construct were far more severe than those of outsiders. Outsiders based their ratings of safety on appearances alone—such things as the presence of vacant buildings, suspicious-looking people hanging around, absence of outdoor activity. They misread some of these cues (for example, they saw a group of men sitting in Market Square as evidence of a friendly community, but residents recognized these men as local winos) and they were unable to draw upon local experience and knowledge (for example, they felt safe in a particular commercial street where residents, who knew of several recent purse snatchings there, felt unsafe). The result was that residents felt safer than outsiders in some places and less safe in others. Residents also recognized greater distinctions between the degree of safety in different places.

We obtained an overall rating for each neighborhood by adding up and averaging the ratings for all ten pictures. (The places shown in the pictures had been identified as characterizing each neighborhood, and so we assumed that taken together the pictures were a reasonable representation of the neighborhood as a whole.) On the whole, residents rated Fells Point more highly than Mount Vernon, and Fells Point residents rated their neighborhood more highly than Mount Vernon residents rated theirs. Outsiders rated Mount Vernon higher than Fells Point; they rated Mount Vernon higher than the people who lived there, and they rated Fells Point lower. How do we explain why residents and outsiders, using the same evaluative constructs, produced different ratings of the two neighborhoods? Could it be that the two groups attached a different order of importance to the individual constructs, and when rating them they applied different standards?

We used the following procedure to find out what importance participants attached to each construct. Participants were asked to indicate the positive pole of each construct, and then they were asked two questions about each positive pole. If, for example, they selected *variety* as the positive pole of a *variety/sameness* construct, they were asked:

A. Just how positive or desirable is variety to you? Would you say it is (1) slightly positive, (2) positive, or (3) very positive?

B. You said that (residents or visitors) like a place that has variety. Would you say that if a place has variety, you (1) may be attracted to it as a place to (live or visit), (2) probably will be attracted to it as a place to (live or visit), or (3) definitely will be attracted to it as a place to (live or visit)?

The mean ratings on these two "importance" questions were used to derive a measure of the strength of each pole. The product of the mean ratings (maximum score $3 \times 3 = 9$) was multiplied by the percentage of participants (100 percent = 1) who had identified the pole as positive. We called this measure the *pole strength* and the maximum score was $3 \times 3 \times 1 = 9$. A higher mean pole strength implied that there was general agreement that that particular quality was more desirable in a place to live or visit.

We found that of the twelve constructs, nine were truly bipolar; that is, there was general agreement, both within and between groups, about which end was positive. For example, 95 percent or more of residents and outsiders agreed that *safe* was a positive quality and *unsafe* a negative one. There was, however, far less agreement on three of the constructs: *complete/changing*, *central/out of the way*, and *quiet/busy*.[7] In the *quiet/busy* construct, for example, about half of the participants chose *quiet* as a positive quality while the other half chose *busy* as a positive quality. Of the 24 qualities in the twelve bipolar constructs, 15 qualities were, then, identified as positive by a significant number of participants. We calculated the mean pole strength of the 15 positive qualities. These are shown in Table 3.1. The level of agreement among participants was taken into account in calculating the pole strength, with the result that nine of the qualities emerge as strong poles, and six as weak ones.

In comparing the importance of the desirable qualities for residents and visitors, we felt it necessary to allow for the possibility of a scale shift between the two groups of raters (that is, residents might have an inherent tendency to be more or less generous in their ratings than outsiders), and so we adjusted the pole strengths to reflect the amount by which each pole strength deviated from the group mean. The adjusted pole strengths for Fells Point are shown in Figure 3.1.

The poles that were rated more highly by residents than by visitors will be referred to as *resident-preferred qualities* and those that were rated more highly by visitors will be referred to as *visitor-preferred qualities*. Resident- and visitor-preferred qualities for each neighborhood are shown below.

Fells Point	Mount Vernon
Resident-preferred qualities	*Resident-preferred qualities*
—	Good for walking
Safe	Safe
Varied	Varied
Many needs	Many needs
Cared for	Cared for
Good looks	Good looks
Complete	—
Quiet	Quiet
Out of the way	—
—	Central
Visitor-preferred qualities	*Visitor-preferred qualities*
Good for walking	—
Interesting	Interesting
Unusual	Unusual
Public	Public
Central	—
Busy	Busy
Changing	Changing
—	Complete
—	Out of the way

Comparing resident-preferred qualities with visitor-preferred qualities in the two neighborhoods, we find disagreement on only four of the fifteen qualities. Three of these—*complete, central,* and *out of the way*—were weak poles, which means that they were of minor importance to both groups. The fourth, *good for walking,* was a strong pole, and the margin of preference by one group over the other was particularly small, which meant that it was of almost equal importance to residents and outsiders.

If one set of priorities is associated with the role of resident and a different set with the role of outsider, then we would expect that an outsider who becomes a resident would switch from one set of priorities to the other; and we would expect the same to be true for a resident who moves away and returns as an outsider. To find out if this was indeed the case, we asked a subsample of residents to play the role of outsiders when rating their own neighborhood, and

Table 3.1   Mean Strength of Each Positive Pole (Maximum strength possible = 9)

	Fells Point		Mount Vernon	
	Residents (n=31)	Visitors (n=22)	Residents (n=31)	Visitors (n=21)
Strong Poles				
Interesting	5.80	7.95	6.31	7.61
Unusual	4.97	6.94	5.66	7.08
Public	2.75	5.37	3.20	5.21
Safe	7.94	5.70	7.81	6.41
Cared for	6.34	4.77	8.40	6.03
Many needs	6.37	5.22	6.72	4.44
Good for walking	7.26	8.23	8.03	7.66
Varied	6.82	6.10	7.12	5.95
Good looking	5.57	5.44	6.74	5.94
Weak Poles				
Complete	2.94	1.96	2.46	2.78
Changing	1.05	2.18	0.75	1.37
Quiet	2.85	1.36	2.75	2.13
Busy	1.84	3.30	2.45	2.46
Central	2.52	3.47	3.18	2.47
Out-of-the-way	1.72	1.17	1.05	1.37
Overall mean	4.44	4.58	4.84	4.59

we asked a subsample of outsiders to rate the strange neighborhood as if they lived there. Then we compared the two sets of responses in each neighborhood.[8]

Let us first consider the responses to the Fells Point pictures. We found that when residents switched roles from resident to outsider, they revised their ratings on all nine primary construct scales, and eight of these revisions were in the direction of the ratings made by "real" outsiders. In the same way, when outsiders pretended to be residents of Fells Point they revised their outsider ratings, and in seven of the nine primary poles these revisions were in the direction of the ratings made by the "real" residents. This ability to see Fells Point from the other point of view means that both groups had a common image of the neighborhood as a place both to live in and to visit (see Figure 3.2).

This was not the case in Mount Vernon. Here residents had trouble seeing it as outsiders, and outsiders had a great deal of trouble seeing it as residents. The two groups did not share a common image of Mount Vernon as they did of Fells Point. Fells Point is, therefore, a better prototype of a balanced resident/outsider environment than Mount Vernon, and a better expression of the qualities that are important in an environment of this type.

Let us now place the findings of the Baltimore study in the context of what we were able to learn from the literature, and return to the question that we asked

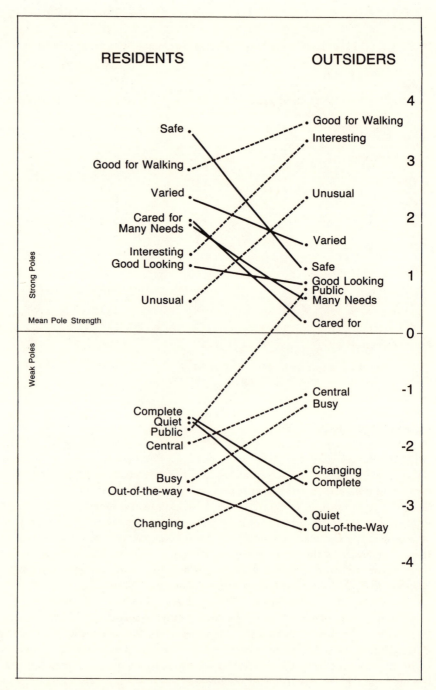

Figure 3.1   Fells Point: Adjusted Pole Strengths

When the importance ratings are plotted, one can see that some qualities were more important to residents and others were more important to outsiders. Illustration by Cynthia Brower.

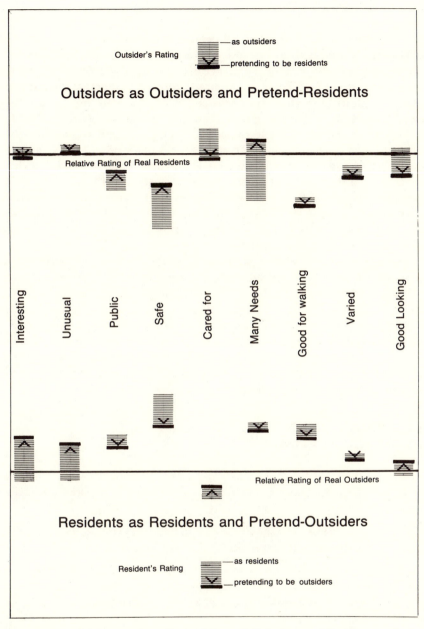

Figure 3.2 Fells Point: Outsiders and Pretend-Outsiders, and Residents and Pretend-Residents

When residents pretended to be outsiders, they shifted their importance ratings in the direction of the ratings given by "real" outsiders (sometimes overshooting the mark). This was true in all nine rating scales. In the same way, when outsiders pretended to be residents, they shifted their importance ratings in the direction of the ratings given by "real" residents. This was true in seven of the nine rating scales. Illustration by Cynthia Brower.

at the beginning of this chapter: how do we define the essential characteristics of places that are good both to live in and to visit?

Looking back at the order of importance of the 15 positive poles (Fig. 3.1), we see that residents of Fells Point and Mount Vernon did not put all the resident-preferred qualities at the top of their list and all the outsider-preferred qualities at the bottom. For example, *good for walking* was an important quality for residents, even though it was less important to them than it was to outsiders. Compared with other studies of satisfaction, residents' scores on some qualities (such as *varied* and *interesting*) were surprisingly high, while on others (such as *quiet* and *out of the way*) their scores were surprisingly low. I believe that these scores reflect concessions that residents made in order to reconcile their interests with those of outsiders. If this explanation is correct, then the priorities of Fells Point and Mount Vernon residents can be translated into guidelines for the design of resident/outsider environments.

The guidelines fall into three categories: those that are generally important in residential settings, those that are more important in resident/outsider than in resident-only settings, and those that are less important in resident/outsider than in resident-only settings. In the following listing, the guidelines in each category are arranged in order of importance, starting with the most important. (Order of importance is not always the same in Fells Point and Mount Vernon. Fells Point is, however, the higher rated residential environment and so I have used it as my model.) To describe each guideline, I have used the words of Fells Point and Mount Vernon residents.

CRITERIA IMPORTANT TO RESIDENTS IN ALL RESIDENTIAL SETTINGS

Safe. One should feel that one is safe and secure. It should be a place that one can go to at any time and not one to avoid. It should not be dark, unfriendly, deserted, or dirty.

Cater to Many Needs. You should be able to find what you need there, and it should be convenient and accessible.

Good Looking. It should be attractive and tasteful, and it should hold together. It should not be ugly, tacky, or cheap looking. It should have character, charm, elegance, a sense of uniformity. It should have attractive buildings and places, textures, shapes, and colors.

(This criterion is something of a catch-all for aesthetic concerns that are not subsumed under the other criteria. Designers will take little comfort from the fact that residents only consider it seventh in the order of priority.)

Well Cared For. It should be clean and looked after, and not rundown or neglected. It should show that people are proud of their neighborhood.

CRITERIA MORE-THAN-USUALLY IMPORTANT TO RESIDENTS IN RESIDENT/OUTSIDER SETTINGS

Good for Walking. It should be pleasant to walk around. One should feel comfortable wandering around. It should encourage strolling. There should be places for sitting.

Varied. There should be different kinds of people and different kinds of buildings and places, and it should reflect a variety of interests and activities. It should not be all the same. There should be different things to see and do, different places to go, and places where different kinds of people can mix.

(In their discussions, participants in Fells Point and Mount Vernon showed an interest in variety and a degree of tolerance for diversity that is not typical of suburban residents. Here are some of the things that they said.)

We don't want to lose our tugs because that's one of the things that makes Fells Point unique. It's a real working community. It's not a showboat place or make-believe place like up at Mystic Seaport. . . .

I think we're really . . . an unusual conglomeration of people, because you have the whole gamut from the street people to the rich people.

I don't really get too upset about the winos because they were here before I was and I knew they were here when I moved here—it didn't keep me away. Sometimes they're fairly funny, other times they're very revolting, but they are a fact of life down here. I guess if I could have one way or the other I would ask that they would find some place else to live, but as a whole they don't bother me.

Interesting Things to See and Do. There should be things going on; places to see, to go to, where one can meet others and be seen; it should be worth making a special trip for. It should be a place one would want to visit, to go inside. One should be able to browse, stroll, hang around, see and participate. It should invite one's curiosity.

Unusual. It should be unique. It should have a distinctive character, such as old-world, picturesque, monumental, or quaint: something that one cannot see just anywhere. It should not be commonplace or ordinary.

Public. It should be open. Strangers should be made to feel welcome and should not be treated like intruders. It should not be personal, restricted, intimate, closed off.

(It is interesting to note that while this was not an important quality (far less important to residents than outsiders), between 70 and 90 percent of resident-participants rated it as a positive quality, and they rated *private* as a negative quality.)

CRITERIA LESS-THAN-USUALLY IMPORTANT TO RESIDENTS IN RESIDENT/OUTSIDER SETTINGS

Complete, Finished. It should be stable, settled, done. It should not look unfinished, in need of rehabilitation, just beginning, or under construction. It should be planned.

Quiet, Peaceful. It should be serene, relaxing, peaceful, a place to get away from it all. It should not be hustle-bustle, congested, busy, hectic, or active.

Out of the Way, Hidden. It should be off the beaten path, on the outskirts of activity. It should not be main street, out in the open, central. It should be a place visitors would pass by.

(The three qualities in this category are generally recognized as desirable in residential areas, and yet they are quite unimportant in Fells Point and Mount Vernon—one third to one half of the resident-participants found them undesirable. This, surely, is a concession to the interests of outsiders.)

In summary, then, I suggest that certain people (because of personal preference, stage in the life cycle, and social circumstances) enjoy living in areas that are varied, interesting, unusual, and accessible to outsiders; and in exchange they are willing to accept an environment that is more public, central, and changeable. While they do not enjoy these outsider-qualities to the extent or to the degree that outsiders do (there were complaints about outsiders' rudeness and thoughtlessness), residents are prepared to reorder their priorities to strike a balance between resident-preferred and outsider-preferred qualities. It does not mean that residents are willing to forgo quiet, seclusion, and continuity, but they do not expect the residential environment to provide these qualities. Instead, they look to the individual house, and they rely on walls, fences, and screens to do what suburban environments do with neighborhood space and a homogeneous user population. The most important resident-preferred criteria are not, however, the things that attract outsiders. Safety, cleanliness, adequacy of services, and overall appearance are as important to residents of resident/outsider neighborhoods as they are to suburbanites.

The studies in Fells Point and Mount Vernon are useful not because they show that people expect different things from in-town neighborhoods than they expect from the suburbs (hardly a surprise), but because they show what these differences are. American cities are experiencing a modest return to in-town living. We should not try to recreate the suburbs downtown, nor should we simply try to recreate there the features we find so delightful in a tour of Barcelona or Chinatown. We must balance the competing interests of residents and outsiders, and the findings in Fells Point and Mount Vernon begin to show what tradeoffs are likely to be made and what are not.

NOTES

1. I looked at eighteen studies. In eight of them participants were asked to evaluate their present neighborhood on the basis of preselected attributes (Galster and Hesser, 1981; Miller et al., 1980; Birch et al., 1977; Campbell, Converse, and Rogers, 1976; Carp, Zawadski, and Shokrkon, 1976; Troy, 1973; Lansing and Marans, 1969; and Munson, 1956). In four studies participants were asked to rate the features of an ideal community (Fried, 1982; Blake, Weigl, and Perloff, 1975; Lamanna, 1964; and Wilson, 1962). One study asked participants to focus on factors that were missing in their neighborhood (Grigsby and Rosenberg, 1975), and one asked about factors which, if they were to change, would reduce neighborhood satisfaction (Winkel, 1981). One study asked participants to evaluate factors that they would consider in choosing a neighborhood (Hinshaw and Allott, 1972), two studies dealt with the factors that made for a good-looking neighborhood (Peterson, 1967; and Nasar, 1983), and one study focused on residents' satisfaction with the quality of local streets (Appleyard, 1981).

2. Fourteen writings were reviewed. They were: Pearce, 1982; Cooper, 1981; Jackson, 1980, pp. 3–9; Zube, 1970, pp. 92–94; Downs and Stea, 1977; Gorman et al., 1977; Nash, 1977; Rapoport, 1977; Smith, 1977; Appleyard, 1976; MacCannell, 1976; Eckbo, 1969; Gans, 1967, pp. 282–283; and Mitford, 1959.

3. This chapter contains selected information from this study. Readers who are in-

	Fells Point	Mount Vernon	Mid-Town Belvedere
Number of residents	2,398	3,206	3,252
white residents	2,165	2,419	2,285
Percent under 15 years	14.5	2.4	3.9
Percent who had never been married or who were separated or divorced	22.8	43.0	43.2
Median age	39.1	31.0	33.6
Median family income	14,223	14,511	14,489
Number of housing units	1,513	2,385	2,769
Percent owners/renters	49.3/50.7	6.4/93.6	5.7/94.3
Percent of residents who had lived there 10 years or more	40.4	10.6	12.9
Percent of residents who had moved in during the preceding 15 months: owners	14.2	9.2	9.6
renters	32.1	43.1	44.3
Median value for specified single-family homes	15,300	74,900	54,700

terested in a full description of the study approach, methodology, and findings, should see the Final Report.

4. The selected census statistics on page 43 were taken from the 1980 Census of Population and Housing published by the U.S. Bureau of the Census. The Fells Point neighborhood that we sampled in the study was somewhat smaller than the area defined by the census, but I believe that the profile is a reasonably representative one. The Mount Vernon area that we sampled incorporated two U.S. census neighborhoods, known as Mount Vernon and Mid-Town Belvedere, and so I include statistics for both areas.

5. Photographs have been used in a number of other studies, and have been found to be reliable proxies for the real thing. See, for example, Lyons, 1983; Shafer and Richards, 1974; Zube, 1974; Seaton and Collins, 1972; and Shafer, Hamilton, and Schmidt, 1969. Using photographs would, we felt, ensure that all participants referred to the same visual images. They could then invest them with their own, personal meanings. For each place we used a set of four pictures taken by different photographers and showing different views. This was done in order to minimize the influence of the photographer. (For discussions about the selection of the scene, see Wartofsky 1980; Wagner, 1979; Becker, 1978 and 1974; Shafer and Richards, 1974; and Byers, 1966 and 1964.) One of the shortcomings of this method was that we could not use images that had meaning for the photographer alone. This meant that we excluded photographs of special people (like friends, a helpful mailman) and eliminated the possibility of eliciting a criterion such as *social desirability*.

6. Our sample of residents was obtained in the following way. Each neighborhood was divided into geographic subareas, and in each subarea we selected a random sample of residents who had listed telephone numbers. We were only able to complete 21 percent of our sample in this way, and so we turned to other ways of obtaining participants.

a. Letters were sent to local institutions, groups and organizations, asking for volunteers. (We obtained 14 percent of the sample in this way.)
b. Notices were placed in local newspapers, asking for volunteers. (We obtained 12 percent of the sample in this way.)
c. Participants were asked, after completing the interview, to refer us to other residents in the neighborhood. (We obtained 52 percent of the sample in this way.) All participants had lived in the neighborhood for at least two years.

From this sample, 27 Fells Point residents were selected at random and asked to respond as residents of Fells Point. Another eight residents of Fells Point were asked to respond as if they were residents of Mount Vernon. Similar groups of Mount Vernon residents were selected in the same way.

Outsiders were obtained in the following way.

a. Nine Fells Point residents were selected at random and asked to respond as outsiders to Mount Vernon, and eight Mount Vernon residents were selected in the same way and asked to respond as outsiders to Fells Point. None of these participants had previously lived in the other neighborhood, and none of them worked there.
b. Eight residents of each neighborhood were selected at random and asked to respond as if they were visitors to their own neighborhood.
c. In addition, eleven out-of-town visitors were interviewed about Fells Point, and the same number were interviewed about Mount Vernon. All were residents of the United States, and none had visited the neighborhood before.

We had, then, a sample design with ten cells, as follows:

Fells Point Residents n=51	Mount Vernon Residents n=52	Out-of-Town Visitors n=22

Responding to Fells Point

1. Residents
   n1=2
   n2=25
2. Play-visitors
   n1=2
   n2=6

3. Play-residents
   n1=2
   n2=6
4. Local visitors
   n1=2
   n2=7

5. Visitors
   n1=2
   n2=9

Responding to Mount Vernon

6. Play-residents
   n1=2
   n2=6
7. Local visitors
   n1=2
   n2=6

8. Residents
   n1=2
   n2=25
9. Play-visitors
   n1=2
   n2=6

10. Visitors
   n1=2
   n2=9

Note: n1 refers to the first interview and n2 to the second.

7. The constructs used by residents and visitors are shown below, and for each construct I show the percentage of participants using that construct who selected each pole as positive.

	Fells Point		Mount Vernon	
	Residents	Visitors	Residents	Visitors
1. Interesting/Not interesting	100/0	100/0	100/0	100/0
2. Unusual/Not unusual	96/4	95/5	100/0	95/5
3. Public/Private	70/30	95/5	90/10	100/0
4. Safe/Unsafe	100/0	100/0	96/4	95/5
5. Cared for/Neglected	93/7	90/10	96/4	100/0
6. Many needs/Few needs	96/4	100/0	96/4	76/24
7. Good for walking/Not good for walking	100/0	100/0	100/0	100/0
8. Varied/Not varied	93/7	100/0	100/0	95/5
9. Good looking/Not good looking	96/4	100/0	96/4	100/0
10. Complete/Changing	64/36	45/54	67/33	71/29
11. Quiet/Busy	59/41	37/63	49/51	43/57
12. Central/Out of the way	51/49	63/37	67/33	66/34

8. The mean neighborhood ratings of residents, visitors, and role-players are shown below. Only the nine strong poles are shown. The maximum score possible is 7.

Fells Point

	Residents	Role-play Visitors*	Visitors**	Role-play Residents***
Interesting	4.87	5.52	4.93	4.82
Unusual	4.92	5.59	5.09	4.92
Public	5.63	5.42	5.06	5.27
Safe	5.52	5.00	4.26	5.00
Cared for	5.10	5.30	5.58	5.00
Many needs	4.33	4.25	3.54	4.60
Good for walking	6.00	5.74	5.27	5.09
Varied	4.67	4.64	4.48	4.24
Good looking	4.95	5.19	5.00	4.54

*   Fells Point residents playing the part of visitors to Fells
     Point.
**   Mount Vernon residents visiting Fells Point.
*** Mount Vernon residents playing the part of residents of Fells
     Point.

Mount Vernon

	Residents	Role-play Visitors*	Visitors**	Role-play Residents***
Interesting	4.86	4.95	5.07	5.27
Unusual	5.02	5.29	5.20	5.75
Public	6.09	5.64	5.47	5.84
Safe	3.53	3.15	4.19	5.54
Cared for	5.34	5.69	5.55	6.29
Many needs	4.02	4.29	3.79	4.59
Good for walking	5.20	5.44	5.39	6.07
Varied	3.63	4.10	3.37	4.80
Good looking	5.21	5.55	5.37	5.94

*   Mount Vernon residents playing the part of visitors to Mount
     Vernon.
**   Fells Point residents visiting Mount Vernon.
*** Fells Point residents playing the part of residents of Mount
     Vernon.

hy these particular forms were chosen—what they tell us about the design-
place in the cosmos, his human and spiritual nature, and his moral and
lectual powers (Norberg-Schulz, 1980). And so, to fully appreciate a design
hould know something about the purposes, circumstances, and religious and
sophical beliefs of the designer. This information cannot alter the quality of
esign, but it makes us better able to understand and interpret it.
his is not the way residents see their residential environment. Residents are
ughly familiar with the place they live in, and consequently they pay less
tion to the surface qualities of the environment and more to what they can
into it[2]; and because their primary interest in the place is as users rather
as observers, they attach less importance to what it says about the human
tion and more to what it says about themselves and their neighbors.
e artistic view, with its emphasis on surface qualities and universal mean-
is more like that of people who are seeing it for the first time than it is of
r users, and this is reflected in designers' frequent references to the percep-
of outsiders—tourists, travellers, and strangers.
te (1945), for example, writes:

ry of travel is the stuff of our fairest dreams. Splendid cities, plazas, monuments,
ndscapes pass before our eyes, and we enjoy again the charming and impressive
cles that we have formerly experienced. (p. 1)

rbusier (1971) describes his city of the future as it would be seen by "[t]he
ler in his airplane, arriving from Constantinople or Pekin" (p. 178).
(1964) describes the qualities that make a city lively by referring to
some diary notes I made on a trip from Naples along the spine of Italy
d Florence" (p. 27). Lynch (1960) asks subjects to draw a map of Boston,
lls them to "Make it just as if you were making a rapid description of the
a stranger, covering all the main features" (p. 141). Cullen (1961) and de
(1966) make frequent references to the experience of visiting a place for
st time; and Jackson (1980) writes of his education, ". . . how seriously
re schooled in how to perceive the world in the traditional tourist man-
p. 7); and of his teaching, he writes, "What I was passing on [to my
ts] were those experiences as a tourist . . . that had been most precious to
. 3).
ress release promoting a new design text reads:

ook] includes original photographs by the author over a fourteen year period of
in England, Spain, Greece, Scandinavia, Japan, Mexico, and the United States.
ts figuratively move back and forth in time and across cultural boundaries to see
n elements of good design. (Kendall/Hunt Publishing Co., 1980)

artistic view, then, is essentially a view from the outside. It relies on first
sions whereas users rely on past experience. Its prototypes of good design
usual places like Venice, Istanbul, Fez, the Greek islands, and Italian hill

---

4

The Subject of Design

Designers look at the environment in a special way, and they see it more
like outsiders than like residents.

In the previous chapter I described a study in which non-designers were shown
pictures of several places in Baltimore, and asked to identify the most distinctive
features of each place. As a supplement to that study, professional designers were
shown the same photographs, and they were given the following instructions:

Please examine each picture carefully and think of it in this way: A client of yours, who is
a developer, gives you this picture and says to you, "This is the kind of place I want you to
design for me." What are the essential features and qualities that you would want to
capture in your design?

Photograph 5 is one of the pictures, and this is the way that designers and non-
designers characterized it[1]:

Designers. Three- and four-story buildings of varied materials, containing offices and
shops, both on the ground floor and one half-story up from the sidewalk. From the
sidewalk you can see into the offices and shops. The buildings are historic, with marble
steps, wrought-iron fences, bay windows and other historical details. They have a scale
that is comfortable for people. They have been renovated and are well kept up. There are
nice show windows and restrained signage. A paved setback creates a zone between the
sidewalk and the building. There are trees on the sidewalk.

Non-Designers. This is a very public place, and one that serves many needs. It is the safest
place in the neighborhood—in fact, it is the only public place that is really safe. It is not

good looking, and it is poorly maintained. There are diffe...
activities.

This paired description exemplifies the difference in...
non-designers looked at the pictures. Designers focused...
color, structure, composition, sightlines, silhouette, an...
while non-designers focused on local significance. Desig...
monumental and exciting, with civic scale, strong de...
sense of wholeness, articulated facades, interesting m...
bience. Non-designers described the same places as s...
good for walking, with plenty to see and do, where on...
place, and where one could go to meet people and be...

As designers, we take an artistic view of the physical...
people respond instinctively to certain physical proport...
nizing, of course, that some peoples' responses are mor...
Objects that incorporate these proportions and patt...
pleasure, and we say that these objects are beauti...
harmonious.

We say that a face is handsome when the precision of the m...
of the features reveal proportions which we *feel to be harmonic*...
within us and beyond our senses, a resonance, a sort of sour...
resonate. (le Corbusier, n.d., p. 203)

A beautiful object or place moves us because of its i...
and so in searching for beauty we must not be distrac...
used for or what it represents, but must see throug...
shapes, textures, tones and colors. Developing an "inn...
major goal of design education. Robert Venturi remer...
tural student, he

went to Europe to look at space and piazzas and spaces bet...
was the equivalent of abstract expressionism. The buildir...
were merely abstract forms making space with textures,...
Beautiful: The Main Street School of Architecture)

Frederick Gibberd (1953) describes a town square in...

We walk into the space in front of the town hall . . . and t...
predominant element—a three-dimensional composition...
houette. Our eye comes down to the normal level . . . a...
attention; we are attracted by the shop fronts, the texture...
sciously register that the snake-like kerb repeats the curve...

The artistic approach recognizes that our response...
ment is not fully explained by a study of proportions...

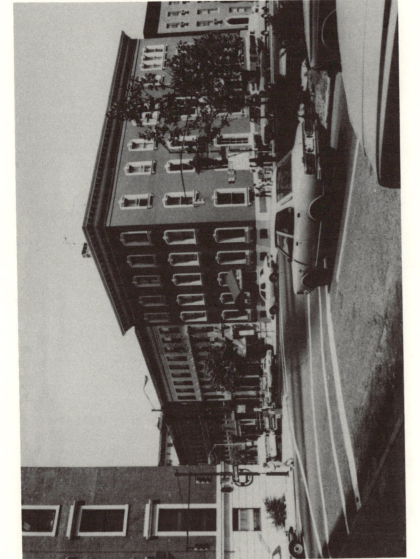

5 Charles Street

Four views of a commercial block on Charles Street were shown to designers and non-designers. This is one of those views.
Photograph by Kate Brower.

towns, never Monte Vista Terrace or Queen Alexandra Lane[3]; and yet unusualness is a quality that fades with frequent exposure and first impressions are superseded in a familiar environment by personal experience and recognition.[4] Designers who rely on the artistic approach will, then, make faulty assumptions about users' perceptions of the environment. For example, Bacon (1967) describes an Italian hill town seen through the eyes of a long-time resident, as a place that is full of surprises:

The form is merely suggested . . . the first flash of impression she receives . . . an entirely new dimension of experience is added by the startling pink walls . . . the view which bursts upon her . . . her anticipation is fulfilled. (pp. 37–41)

This is an unlikely description. A structured sequence of surprises can tantalize and allure a stranger, but not someone who has been there many times before and who knows exactly what lies ahead. Moreover, one seldom appreciates being surprised in one's home environment where the very purpose of familiarization has been to make the environment predictable (Kaplan and Kaplan, 1982, p. 63; Appleyard, 1976, p. 215). One cannot attribute to a resident one's own responses as an outsider-designer.[5]

I remember when, several years ago, a Baltimore sculptor was commissioned to design innovative play equipment for an inner city playground. The City wanted to do something special. Several residents of the neighborhood, interviewed by a local television station at the opening ceremony, complained that the City had once again chosen the poor to experiment on. Why couldn't they get a regular playground like everyone else?

Le Corbusier's workers' houses in Pessac were known throughout the design community for their pure, simple forms, and as monuments to a new style. To the residents of Pessac, however, the houses looked Moroccan, and this carried a social stigma. A resident commented:

It was as if we had the plague: What! you live in the "Moroccan District!" (Boudon, 1972, p. 15)

In his designs for low cost housing in Egypt, Fathy (1973) experimented with mud brick construction and was able to produce a series of vaulted and domed spaces that were low in cost, efficient, and climate-sensitive; they were also attractive, with pure forms and clean lines. He used this system to build housing for rural peasants, but he discovered that the peasants disliked the buildings because they associated mud bricks with hovels, and vaulted roofs with tombs. They preferred Western-style, prefabricated buildings, which they saw as progressive, but Fathy saw as inappropriate and ugly.

In all of these instances, local meanings that played an important part in the residents' perceptions were not taken into account in the design process. Still, designers seldom have firsthand experience of the places they design. How would they know how local residents interpret features of the environment?

The most direct way to see an environment as residents do is to imagine ourselves in their place, and to draw on our experience of places where we ourselves have lived. In situations not covered by our experience—where we do not know enough about the lifestyle and values of a particular group of residents—we must read, discuss, interact, and observe their behavior.[6] We can also learn a great deal by looking at the physical environment. When the original architecture (that is, the relatively fixed features of house and neighborhood, such as lot size; size, type, form and style of buildings; and the character and mix of uses) represents a deliberate choice and a substantial investment on the part of the residents, it is usually a reliable indicator of such things as social structure, culture, history, and prevailing standards.[7]

Impermanent features of the environment also tell us about the things that residents think are important. Residents' additions, corrections, and modifications to the architecture—cutting the grass, making structural changes, fixing, cleaning, and decorating—can tell us a great deal about their values, social class, commitments, attachments, interests, and feeling of security. Features that are inexpensive to produce and require regular reaffirmation (repairing, replanting, or refurbishing) give us the most topical and current information about residents. In gentrifying neighborhoods, for example, the architecture remains essentially unchanged, but the impermanent features tell of a change in the population (Hanson and Hillier, 1982; Thompson, 1979):

The [middle class resident] makes his early Victorian house older by fitting a six-panel Georgian front door with exact reproduction brass door furniture from Beardmore's and painting it either a classic dull colour such as Adam Gold or Thames Green or, better still, black and white. His [working class] neighbour makes his house younger by flushing the original four-panel door with hardboard, fitting pressed steel or brushed aluminum door furniture such as one would find on a modern private estate and in the local hardware shop, and painting it in a contemporary bright color such as Canary Yellow or Capri Blue. (Thompson, p. 48)

Residents are particularly sensitive to signs of care as a source of local information[8]:

On Calvert Street the row houses stood in two endless lines. "I don't see how you knew which one was home," Luke had told him once, and Cody had been amazed. Oh, if you lived here you knew. They weren't all alike, not really. One had dozens of roses struggling in its tiny front yard, another an illuminated madonna glowing night and day in the parlor window. Some had their trim painted in astonishing colors, assertively, like people with their chins thrust out. The fact that they were *attached* didn't mean a thing. (Tyler, 1982, pp. 281–282)

In low income areas, where people cannot afford to be picky about the architecture of their houses or their neighborhood, and where care represents serious choices and involves relatively large investments of time and money, personal attention, compromise, and improvisation, signs of care can be considerably more revealing than the architecture.

Because impermanent features affect the appearance of the environment, designers cannot ignore them. It would be convenient if we could build them into the basic design, but we can never give them the authenticity that residents can. It is possible, however, to create conditions under which particular features are likely to be generated. We can do this because there is an order and logic to the social conventions that define settings for different patterns of behavior.

There are, then, two approaches to design. The artistic approach takes the view of the outsider and directs attention to observers' responses; the local approach takes the view of the insider and directs attention to users' inferences. The two approaches represent different modes of perceiving the environment. Each creates a different context for design decisions. Both are the proper subject of design. Kevin Lynch expressed it best:

In the past, the consideration of sense has been based solely on an analysis of the physical environment. Concepts such as harmony, beauty, variety and order have been thought of as attributes of the thing itself. Designers have unconsciously relied on their own implicit values and perceptions, projecting them on the physical world as if they were inherent qualities. Not so—one begins with the images and priorities of the users of a place and must look at place and person together. (Lynch, 1981, p. 150)

Despite Lynch's admonition, it is not general practice for designers to look at place and person together. Many of us look only at place. We are encouraged to take the outsider view because designs that satisfy users do not necessarily satisfy other designers, who look at them, quite naturally, as outsiders do. Few design awards are won because a project looks new, feels safe, make outsiders feel out of place, or encourages good maintenance. When working in residential areas, we also find that our own desire to innovate is at odds with residents' innate conservatism.[9] Georges Maurios (1984), the architect for a new apartment house, invited prospective residents to design their own individual units within the building. He expected that the results would be innovative and unusual. Maurios found, however, that given the opportunity to create personal environments, residents chose to recreate familiar ones.

Ironically perhaps, most families' interest in our experiment . . . did not consist so much in the possibility of changing their way of life, but in the possibility of continuing a way of life established in an earlier dwelling. (p. 68)

Residents' conservatism when it comes to their home environment explains, perhaps, why so many houses associated with the avant-garde movement in architecture have been guest houses, or vacation or second homes.

NOTES

1. Designers and non-designers were responding to exactly the same pictures. The method of presentation was somewhat different in that non-designers were shown three pictures at a time and asked to identify a "quality that is especially important to a resident (or visitor) that you can see in two of the pictures but not in the third," while designers were shown the pictures one at a time and asked to identify "the essential features and qualities that you would want to capture in your design." I believe that the two sets of instructions produced comparable results. For details of the study methodology and findings, see Brower, 1985.

2. Appleyard (1976) found that long-time residents attached more importance to the significance of buildings and places than newcomers did.

As knowledge develops, significance deepens: social patterns, historic events, and functional meanings are interpreted through the visible environment. The trend is away from the powerful (surface) imagery of the earlier period. (p. 215)

Others have also written about the effect of increasing familiarity on environmental perception. See for example, Kaplan and Kaplan, 1982, p. 123; Lynch 1981, p. 132; Downs and Stea, 1977, p. 248; and Lowenthal, 1975. It has often been noted that visitors and residents do not look for the same visual features. See for example, Lynch, 1981, p. 160; Steele, 1981, p. 248; Rapoport, 1977, p. 374; Lansing and Marans, 1969; and Gans, 1967, p. 186.

3. Jackson (Zube, 1970), taking a visitor's-eye-view of the suburbs, is conscious of the lack of novelty.

As one who is by way of being a professional tourist . . . many are the hours I have spent wandering through carefully labyrinthine suburbs, seeking to discover the *essential* city, as distinguished from that of the tourist or transient. In retrospect, these districts all seem indistinguishable: tree- and garden-lined avenues and lanes, curving about a landscape of hills with pretty views over other hills; the traffic becomes sparser, the houses retreat further behind tall trees and expensive flowers; every prospect is green, most prosperous and beautiful. Yet why have I always been so glad to leave? Was it a painful realization that I was excluded from these rows and rows of (presumably) happy and comfortable homes that has always ended by making me beat a retreat to the city proper? Or was it a conviction that I had actually seen this, experienced it, relished it after a fashion countless times and could no longer derive the slightest spark of inspiration from it? . . . The residential quarter, despite its undeniable charms, is not the entire city, and if we poor lonely travellers are ignorant of the joys of existence on Monte Vista Terrace and Queen Alexandra Lane we are on the other hand apt to know much more about some other aspects of the city than the life-long resident. I am thinking in particular of that part of the city devoted to the outsider. . . . (Zube, 1970, pp. 92–93)

Herbert Gans (1967) comments that design critics' aversion to the suburbs is based on the fact that they see them as tourists rather than residents.

Much of the critique of suburbia as community reflects the critics' disappointment that the suburbs do not satisfy their particular tourist requirements; that they are not places for wandering, that they lack the charm of a medieval village, the excitement of a metropolis . . . (p. 186)

4. Csikszentmihalyi and Rochberg-Halton (1981) found that even paintings in the home were enjoyed for their associations rather than their artistic qualities.

Thus the bulk of significations carried by visual "works of art" is not connected to aesthetic values and experiences but refers to the immediate life history of their owners: reminding them of relatives or friends or past events. People pay particular attention to pictures in their home because in doing so they relive memorable occasions and pleasing relationships. (p. 65)

5. A number of studies have tried to measure differences in perception between designers and non-designers. Typically, two groups—designers (usually architectural students) and non-designers—were shown identical pictures of buildings and asked to rate each picture on preselected adjective rating scales such as cheerful, ordered, and strong (see, for example, Hershberger, 1971), or sad/happy, discordant/harmonious, and rugged/delicate (see, for example, Nasar and Kunawong, 1987; Canter, 1969); or they were asked to rate each picture on a preference scale: How do you like it? (Kaplan, Dale, and Kaplan, 1987). The results of these studies are indecisive: for example, Hershberger found pronounced differences between architects and non-architects, while Nasar and Kunawong did not. The absence of quantitative measures does not, however, mean that differences in perception do not exist.

6. For different ways of studying unfamiliar environments, see Meier, 1980; Meinig (ed.), 1979; Appleyard, 1979a; Clay, 1973.

7. In a study by Cherulnik and Wilderman (1986), college students were shown eighteen photographs of nineteenth century houses in Boston. Some of the houses had been designed for upper-class clients and some for lower. The houses represented variations in architectural detail rather than in use and condition. The photographs were assessed by two groups of subjects. One group had a list of occupations and the other had a list of personal traits. Participants were asked to look at each building and select eight words from their list that best described the building's occupants. The results showed that the houses originally designed for the upper classes were most frequently identified with insurance agents, lawyers, doctors, judges, accountants, and airline pilots; and their occupants were characterized as neat, intelligent, proud, energetic, ambitious, materialistic, and outgoing. In contrast, the houses originally designed for the lower classes were most frequently seen as the homes of truck drivers, laundry workers, cooks, janitors, waiters, and auto mechanics; and their occupants were characterized as timid, thrifty, superstitious, gullible, irresponsible, lazy, and noisy.

8. The meaningfulness of resident-generated improvements has been noted in several sociological studies. See, for example, Gans' (1967) comments about residents' perceptions of Levittown:

[Residents'] image of other houses was determined not by their facades, but by their occupants, so that (for neighbors at least) every house quickly became unique. None of the adults who thought Levittown dull ascribed the dullness to architectural homogeneity. (p. 282)

Wilmott (1963) comments on the appearance of resident-generated features in an English housing project:

The first view is of endless thoroughfares lined with straight rows of identical houses . . . The net impression is of street after street of houses, mile upon mile of them.

It is not until one begins to look more closely at what people have done to the houses that the impression of sameness recedes a little. The place has 'weathered'; the tenants and time have between them taken off that raw look of new council housing. Homes . . . give the appearance of thousands of hands having smoothed over, and made more human, the original plans rolled out from County Hall. (p. 4)

9. Lewis (1975) notes that immigrants recreate familiar house-types of the old country even though they may be quite unsuited to the new conditions:

. . . technological innovations [do not] ordinarily have much effect on the form of common houses. Innovations, after all, are likely to make one's house look funny. . . . [N]ew building technology gains quickest adoption in the design of factories, warehouses, and schools, where efficiency counts but looks do not. (p. 2)

5

Design Conventions

Behavior settings have physical and human components. These components and the relationship between them are governed by social conventions, and designers and users both operate within these conventions.

There are conventions that define what is appropriate and what is inappropriate in, for example, a house, church, school, store, playground, yard, alley, or street. These conventions apply both to the physical environment (its form and appearance) and to the behavior of those who use it (how they use it, and arrangements for the ongoing operation and maintenance of the use). Successful spaces and facilities conform to the conventions of the particular society to which the users belong; they owe their success not simply to the way they look, but to the way they are used, managed, presented, and interpreted, and to the goodness of fit between their physical and behavioral components. They function as behavior settings.[1] To illustrate, consider the case of outdoor festivals.

Festivals are a traditional form of public celebration. They appear almost overnight, are there for a brief period of time, and then are gone; and they appear and reappear in much the same form and often in the same location and at regular intervals so that, like the mythical village of Brigadoon, we can think of them as temporal as well as material landscapes.

Between mid-April and the end of November 1975, information was collected about more than three hundred outdoor festivals in Baltimore.[2] The list, by no means complete, included the City Fair, an arts festival, several ethnic festivals, and a multitude of block parties, bazaars, fairs, carnivals, marts, parades, and sales. The events were organized by non-profit corporations, neigh-

6   Territories

This urban space is divided into private yards, a communal alley, and a public street. Each parcel serves a different set of users and uses, and is governed by different conventions. Photograph courtesy of Baltimore City Department of Planning.

borhood associations, merchants, block groups, churches, political organizations, charities, service agencies, promotion councils, scout troops, social clubs,
and school PTAs. They were organized for many purposes: to raise money, to
impart information, to publicize local issues, to promote a particular locality, to
exhibit aspects of a particular heritage. An underlying theme was the desire to
bring people together and to reinforce group solidarity, all in the spirit of fun.

The festivals varied enormously in size. The City Fair was a three-day extrava-
ganza that attracted more than a million people; other events drew from 70
thousand to less than a hundred people. Whatever their size, however, all the
festivals drew from a common vocabulary of offerings. You could be sure to find
pizza at the Italian Festival, but you might also find it at an arts festival, a church
bazaar, and a block party. Most festivals had hot dogs, sodas, and baked goods.
Many had rides. None of the offerings were really peculiar to festivals: whatever
it was you bought there you could have bought with greater ease and convenience somewhere else. The festivals had many of the features of a commercial
enterprise and yet one of the most damning things that could be said about a
festival was that it was commercial. This is because festivals were governed not
by the conventions of commerce but by the conventions of play.

Huizinga (1955) defined six conventions of play, and as the following descriptions show, these six conventions explain the special physical and behavioral
qualities of festivals.

1.   *Play is a voluntary activity, something that one does for enjoyment
and not because one has to.*

The vast majority of people who worked on the festivals were volunteers,
some with highly professional organizational skills. Festival-going was, of course,
voluntary. People were attracted to different festivals for different reasons; for
example, the City Fair was unrivaled for its scale and variety, open house tours
offered a glimpse into other people's personal lives, ethnic festivals provided
some of the exotic quality of an overseas vacation, and neighborhood festivals
allowed neighbors to celebrate some of the elements that held them together.
But people did not go to a festival with a particular purpose in mind; they came
to look around, see what was there, open themselves to the joys of serendipity.
They might find a bargain, see something unusual, run into a friend, or meet
someone new. The opportunity for exploration and discovery did not show up in
any list of featured events and offerings, but if it were absent, many people would
not have gone to festivals.

When asked the best features of a festival, most people referred to the joyful
atmosphere, and they described it in the following words: congenial, friendly,
togetherness, good attitudes, full of spirit, nice people, having a good time,
sincerity, smiles, pretty girls, good-looking boys, love in the air, kind people,
happy people, 'good vibes'. There was a happy relationship among people at
festivals, and for most people the quality of this relationship was the measure of a
good festival.

7 Baltimore Festival

Dressing up is a clear sign that the activity is apart from the real, everyday world. Photograph by Alain Jaramillo.

8   Baltimore Festival

Dressing-up is a clear sign that the activity is apart from the real, everyday world. Photograph by Alain Jaramillo.

*2.   Play is bounded in time and space: the action takes place in a
particular place and at a particular time; it begins and then, at a certain
moment, it is over. But it is remembered, transmitted, and repeated; in
fact, repetition is one of the most essential elements of play.*

The City Fair and several of the larger festivals were held downtown, but the
vast majority of festivals were held in the neighborhoods: in local parks and
playgrounds, on the grounds of a school, hospital or church, in alleys, vacant
lots, parking lots, backyards, and most frequently in streets that had been
temporarily closed to traffic. These spaces were transformed, almost overnight,
with the impermanent trappings of a festival: barricades, booths, banners,
stages, bandstands, balloons, tents, and mechanical rides. The festival lasted for
a predetermined time, and when it was over all the paraphernalia was gone.

Most organizers felt that their festival should be repeated; and in fact, most
festivals were repeated every year, often in the same location, and many people
attended the same festival year after year.[3] Repetition did not guarantee continuity, but it increased the likelihood that the festival would be held again the
following year because it was more likely to have gained a reputation, a tradition, and a following.

*3.   There is an internal order, a set of rules that holds together the
temporary world of play. Any deviation from these rules "spoils the
game", robs it of its character, and makes it worthless.*

Among the worst features of festivals were slow service, long lines, crowds,
and a shortage of seating. What was surprising was that festival-goers were
prepared to tolerate so much discomfort and inconvenience, and they did it in
the spirit of fun and goodwill. What really bothered festival-goers was the
thought that the festivals were becoming commercialized: that some people were
treating them as a "serious" business, something that was run to make a profit.

*4.   Play incorporates an element of uncertainty and tension; and the play
involves a striving to decide an issue, to succeed, to win.*

Festival organizers had a great deal of work to do. They had to set the time
and location, secure the site, acquire sponsors, raise money, enlist helpers,
obtain permits, contract with entertainers and food vendors, mount a publicity
campaign, arrange for exhibits, booths, stands, deliveries, power supply, parking, ticket sales, security, and clean-up. They depended on donations, volunteers, and good weather, all of which involved a good deal of risk and the only
thing you could count on was that the unexpected would happen. The result was
that decisions were often made on the spur of the moment and often changed,
and there was a general air of hysteria that would have been unbearable if one
had thought of it as work. But organizers did not think of the festival as work.
They saw it as a challenge, a risk that they could never afford in their work; it
was a test of their ingenuity and imagination, their ability to do the impossible.

Organizers found it difficult to describe the ideal festival site because the ideal site was one with inherent obstacles that they could overcome.

5. *Players in a game have the sense of sharing something important, and of being different from those who are not in the game. This difference is most vividly expressed in dressing-up.*

People at festivals had a tendency to dress up in national costumes, fancy dress, novelty clothes, funny hats, stage make-up, and masks: trappings from the world of make-believe. Things that would look ridiculous in the serious everyday world were in place in a festival. People at festivals were themselves on display.

Festival organizers developed a strong feeling of camaraderie, and when they spoke about one another, they spoke of cheerfulness, helpfulness, enthusiasm, and friendliness.

6. *Play is an interlude in our daily lives rather than a part of it. It belongs to one's "spare time" and to the realm of make-believe rather than reality.*

The playful quality of a festival was reflected in people's actions. There was a general understanding that what one did during a festival had no bearing on everyday life, and as a result there was a good deal of eccentric, idiosyncratic, and provocative behavior. Traditional expectations and customary social boundaries were suspended, and performances, commitments, and concessions made during a festival had no currency once the festival was over. One was free to experiment with minimal risk, and so one found corporate executives being supervised by blue-color workers, politicians trying their hand as auctioneers or counterhands, people on the social register working side by side with people on the welfare roll.

Festivals usurped a space that was assigned to other uses, and disrupted its normal functions. But festivals were not seen as a threat to the "real" occupants of the site because they were not a "serious" use. The play status of festivals was clearly reflected in the physical elements that were blatantly temporary and playful. This makeshift quality was an important feature of the festival: it meant that the festival was not there to stay. It conveyed an impression of guilelessness and spontaneity, and gave the feeling that what one saw at a festival was not carefully staged, that it was authentic. A festival was not the real world, but it was unusually revealing of it.

The impermanence of the play trappings has special importance for those who play on home ground. A familiar place embodies the routines and responsibilities associated with day-to-day living; play paraphernalia have the effect of changing the appearance of the site, loosening the grip of past associations, and liberating the players from their everyday concerns; and this is a signal to take "time out," to play. But the effect of these changes is necessarily shortlived, because as novelty fades, the play objects themselves become familiar and lose their magic. The fact that an environment has constantly to be remade does not destroy its playfulness, and the fact that it is tacky does not destroy its festive quality. Success ultimately depends on whether the activity is in accordance with the spirit of play.

Social play takes different forms. Some forms of play, such as festivals, are carefully planned and organized, but other forms are spontaneous and random. In some residential areas, for example, window displays (arrangements of vases, figurines, knickknacks, artificial flowers, mottos, awards, cards, photographs, posters and paper cut-outs) are used to celebrate family milestones, holidays, anniversaries, and seasonal events. In an interview reported in *The Sun* newspaper ("Bricolage", 1987), one resident explains that she

. . . decorates her windows for almost every holiday—Halloween, Thanksgiving, Valentine's Day, Easter, the Fourth of July and opening day of the Orioles' season at Memorial Stadium. But Christmas is when she and her husband really do it up. At this most festive time of the year, they decorate the basement windows as well.

This type of window decoration (see Photograph 9) is a form of play and it conforms to the appropriate conventions of play: it is voluntary, a spare-time activity, bounded in place and time, with an internal order (Santa Claus at Christmas, Indian corn on Thanksgiving, Stars and Stripes on Flag Day, Bunny at Easter); it involves an element of competition (many communities offer prizes for the best display), and engenders a sense of camaraderie with the other players in the game (often whole blocks of houses are decorated and the decorations are coordinated). This playful activity is a response to a social occasion, but it is facilitated by the physical features of the environment—one seldom finds decorations in windows that face away from the street or are higher than the third floor.

Sometimes play transformations occur in the conceptual rather than the physical world. This is more characteristic of children than it is of adults, because children's perceptions are fresher, their imagination is more active, and what they imagine seems more real: an eggcrate on the sidewalk is a spacecraft on its way to Mars, or a bridge over the Amazon. Barker and Wright (1951) described a day in the life of a seven-year-old boy. Their account of the journey to school included the following sequence of events: the boy tipped up a park bench on the courthouse lawn, vaulted over it, and then balanced on the top, played an imaginary game of baseball, repeatedly hit a metal flagpole with a bat to make ringing noises, walked while turning around in circles, climbed up and walked along the top of a retaining wall, sat down and rocked on a bench, examined some pieces of rubber tubing in the road, jumped up and down, looked in the store window, walked along a ledge, and kicked in the dust. A familiar street became a temporary play place and everyday objects were transformed into temporary playthings.

Perhaps the most important thing that a designer can learn from a study of play is that a play setting is not the same thing as a play space. Just as play can

9   Window Decorations

Christmas decorations are an expression of social play. Photograph by the author.

occur in the absence of a special facility, the provision of a special facility does not necessarily mean that play will happen there—a fact that should be evident from widespread reports of underutilized playgrounds.[4] Designing conditions suitable for play sometimes means programs and physical elements that facilitate temporary transformations, rather than specialized, permanent play equipment or exclusive play places. In Baltimore's Play-Street program, for example, neighborhood streets were temporarily closed to automobile traffic, and a fun-wagon moved in to transform the street into a playground. The wagon offered basketball, volleyball, frisbee, jump rope, trampoline, table tennis, pool, spin top, bikeorama, and sprinkler units. After a few hours all the equipment was removed and the street opened once again to traffic. But the play setting returned one day a week during the summer months. In addition to the fun-wagon, the City had other mobile units: a crafts wagon, skatemobile, sidewalk theater, and marionette show. These mobile programs generated play with only incidental, temporary effects on the physical environment, and at the same time that nearby playgrounds with permanent play equipment were deserted.

In designing for play, then, program may be every bit as important as place or equipment. Even the Baltimore festivals, despite their air of spontaneity, did not "just happen": the City had a program through which neighborhood groups could obtain (at no charge) booths, stages, tables, toys, games, theatrical performances, music and dance groups, exhibits, and demonstrations. The City also provided loudspeaker systems, publicity, advice on layout and graphics, and special security, sanitation, and traffic control services.[5]

In all forms of play the lighthearted activity may hide serious purposes: it promotes the health and growth of the individual and the expression, interpretation, and development of culture (Huizinga, 1955; Chase, 1977). Play is an opportunity to experiment with new social roles, strengthen community ties, and celebrate and transmit cultural values. Because play involves the suspension of normal patterns of behavior, it is an excellent vehicle for introducing new behaviors. Marketing people are well aware of this fact, and they win new customers for products and services ranging from food to education by presenting them as "fun". Play can also be used to change regular behavior in public places. This is illustrated by the Clean-Block competition in Baltimore. The Clean-Block competition, which offers prizes for the best looking street block, has been run every summer since the 1930s, with only a few interruptions, by the Afro-American newspaper. Any city block can enter the competition (although in fact the blocks that do enter are all in inner-city, low-income, predominantly black neighborhoods). All that is needed is an application signed by the residents of the block. A panel of judges inspects each of the competing blocks, and makes awards based on the degree of improvement that has taken place over the period of the competition. After the final judging there is an official prize-giving; the prizes include money (which usually goes for a block party) and public recognition in the form of banners for the street, decals for the windows, and pictures in the newspaper. The results are quite startling. People paint their housefronts, sidewalks, and curbs; they bring out furniture, ornaments and planters; and they clean the streets, sidewalks, alleys, and yards. The block acquires a festive quality.

The sponsors of the Clean-Block competition have a serious purpose: they hope that (in addition to selling more newspapers) short-term changes in public behavior and the residential environment will have long-term effects. They could have appealed to a sense of responsibility and civic duty, but they realised that people will do things in the spirit of play that they will not do when it is demanded of them. The Clean-Block competition conforms to the conventions of play: it is voluntary, it is not necessary, it occurs in a defined place and time and is repeated every year, it has rules, players compete to win, and it engenders a team spirit. Above all, it is fun.

Just as there are conventions that govern play settings, there are conventions that govern residential settings. Residential conventions are based on occupancy type, each occupancy type characterized by a particular set of rights and responsibilities associated with use and control. If we change an occupancy type, even if we stick to the same physical locale, different physical elements and different sets of behavior become acceptable and appropriate. I should like to illustrate this by describing four scenarios for the same locale. Choosing the locale presents a problem because most occupied places are associated with particular types of occupancy, which means that unfamiliar scenarios will seem more far-fetched and less credible than familiar ones. To overcome this problem I have chosen a locale that is not customarily associated with occupancy at all: an underground cavern. In each case I will outline the key conventions associated with a particular occupancy, and will then describe the caverns as they might appear if they conform to those conventions. While the descriptions are somewhat fanciful they illustrate four common occupancy types: personal, community, general, and free occupancies.[6]

PERSONAL OCCUPANCY

Conventions Associated with Personal Occupancy

Personal occupancies are controlled by individuals and groups whose members have clear and lasting relationships, and whose primary ties and loyalties are to one another. The most common examples are groups in which members are bound by blood or marriage. The single-family house is a prototype of this type of occupancy. Personal occupancies are accorded the greatest freedom of any occupancy type to restrict admission and to control use. Regulations will be accepted even if they appear to be selfish, whimsical, or illogical, and without demanding justification, consistency, or advance notice, as long as they are not unduly antisocial. The signs of personal occupancy have private rather than general significance, and are strongest if they are associated with the person of the occupants—their visible presence; display of family photographs, diplomas,

10   Afro Clean-Block Winner

Note the way the curb, steps and planters have been painted in matching colors. Next year the residents will do something different. Photograph by Alain Jaramillo.

and souvenirs; memories of important events. Personal occupancies seldom cater to the convenience of strangers, but they can be very solicitous of guests.

The Caverns as Personal Occupancy

On leaving our car at the lodge, we proceed directly to the main house and on presenting our card to the butler, we are ushered into a study where our host awaits us. After a short exchange of politenesses, he takes us on a tour of his well-known caverns.

The large hall of the caverns is entered directly from the study by means of a wooden staircase. As we pass underneath the staircase, we are alarmed to notice that the supporting timbers are in a state of near collapse and that the treads themselves are rotting and decayed. Our host, much delighted by our evident alarm, informs us that the rotting timbers are in fact an illusion, a mock-up which he has had prepared as a joke for the amusement of his friends. We proceed along a narrow passage and arrive at the central cavern. The cavern has been fashioned into a banquet hall, complete with main table and benches carved out of stone. We are urged to try the seats, and when we do so we are sprayed by fine jets of water set into the stone faces of the seats and the table edge. Our host is much amused, and regales us with tales of others' reactions. Not all the caverns are open for inspection: one is used as a wine cellar (the temperature and humidity being most suitable) and several others are used for storage purposes. One of the passages, we notice, has been walled up. This must surely be the passage that led to the chamber with the small rock pool where, it is whispered, our host's unhappy wife drowned her infant son before shooting herself. The other caverns that we enter are illuminated and decorated with much imagination and originality.

At the conclusion of the tour we return to the study where our host serves tea from a large silver teapot. We thank him and head back to the car. On our way, we discover that a row of water jets has been buried on either side of the path.

COMMUNITY OCCUPANCY

Conventions Associated with Community Occupancy

Community occupancies are controlled by groups whose composition may change, but whose members have undergone a common screening process, and frequently initiation rites. These serve to establish a clear and consistent distinction between group members and outsiders; a distinction sometimes expressed through special costume, ritual, language, and references. Eligibility as a member of a community may depend upon sharing a physical setting (a neighborhood group), a system of values or beliefs (a church congregation), a climate of benefit or risk (co-workers) or, as is frequently the case, a combination of these things. The organization of the group may depend largely upon informal understandings, but a structured relationship will be more effective in dealing with outsiders. Places in community occupancy are allowed less freedom than those in personal occupancy. While a wide range of restrictions and controls are acceptable, they must fall clearly within the framework of the community purpose, and must conform to the common practices and established traditions of the larger society. The signs of community occupancy derive from the practical and symbolic needs of its members. They remind members of common interests, and they frequently have strong esoteric overtones (such as signs, badges, and logotypes) that serve to impress upon outsiders the exclusionary nature of the occupancy.

The Caverns as Community Occupancy

On leaving our car at the monastery door, we proceed through the garden to the small chapel where we receive the traditional benediction from a tonsured member of the order. He leads us to the cavern mouth in the hillside. The entrance cavern has been fashioned into a small shrine, the altar cut from the living rock, and a stalactite has been ingeniously and painstakingly carved and fitted to form a lantern. Through a heavy oak door we enter the passage and beyond it we find a succession of chambers that have served for several centuries as burial crypts for members of the monastic sect. We wander past grotesque mounds of bones, trying to decifer ancient inscriptions and to guess at the identity of the men whose sculptured busts look down on us with empty eyes. The cavern formations tower up as guardians of this strange scene.

The main hall has a small rock pool in the center, the water of which is slightly salty to the taste. It is said that the sainted founder of the monastic order had discovered the cavern one day when seeking shelter from an approaching storm. While in the cavern, he began to contemplate the sins of mankind and was so immersed in his meditations that he did not notice the storm pass but sat for three days and three nights without moving, weeping all the while. He tears filled the hollow stone and by some miracle they remain undiminished through the years. Many of the small caverns have been fashioned into shrines and it is in one of these that the now celebrated "Madonna of the Caves" is to be seen. Our guide tells us of the early history of the monastery and of the many strange events that these caverns have witnessed.

When we return to the dazzling light of day we are presented with a glass of the famous monastery brandy, and in appreciation for the kindness shown us, contribute a small sum of money toward a fund for repairing the roof of the refectory building.

GENERAL OCCUPANCY

Conventions Associated with General Occupancy

General occupancies are controlled by the public. They may include some places that are publicly owned (a street) but not others (a pumping station), and may include many places that are not publicly owned (a movie theater, or the mall in a shopping center). General occupancies are accorded less freedom to restrict admission and control use than either personal or community occupancies. They do not, however, have to be equally accessible to all members of the public, so long as the restrictions conform to the prevailing customs of society. In this way, there may be differences based on sex (women are not allowed to use men's bathrooms) or age (some stores exclude schoolchildren during school hours). Both the nature of controls and the measures for enforcement of controls will vary from one society to another. Enforcement is frequently entrusted to public officials who wear familiar uniforms or badges. The signs used to identify occupancies by society are explicit, clear, legible, and standardized. They are designed to serve as guides for the uninitiated.

The Caverns as General Occupancy

On leaving our car in the large parking lot, we follow the signs to the modern structure that covers the entrance to the caverns. Tickets are available at the desk, and a loud-speaker announces that the next tour will begin in twenty-three minutes.

We follow our guide along a level, well-lit passage and emerge in the entrance cavern, the "Jefferson Hall." There is a prominent notice asking us please to refrain from smoking or littering the cavern floors. The guide gives us a brief history of the caverns and points out the rough passage which formed the original access to the caverns. He also points out "Nature's Barometer," a small rock pool in the center of the hall and tells of the narrow underground connection between the pool and a surface lake in an adjacent valley. The water level in the pool rises and falls, exaggerating major fluctuations of the lake surface, thus indicating changes in outside air pressure.

Our guide leads us along "Webster Avenue" through a succession of caverns. The paths are paved in brick and are lined with guard rails, grades are eased and ramped or stepped, chasms are bridged, the illumination is good, and the major formations are signposted. As the path traces the form of a figure "S", we return to the entrance hall along "Corcoran Avenue" so that we have not had to retrace our steps—a feature of this particular cavern development. (A rival cavern features elevator service.) We return to the shelter at the far end of the curio shop, which we have to traverse to get to the restaurant.

FREE OCCUPANCY

Conventions Associated with Free Occupancy

Free occupancies have no established occupants, and are subject to the rules and restrictions of no particular person or group. The rules that guide behavior are self-imposed, or else they are attributed to supernatural forces or common decency. Free occupancies are characterized by the absence of man-made signs (especially signs such as official warnings that imply that someone is in charge); they invite exploration and excite the imagination. They can be exhilarating. They can also be terrifying. Deserted beaches and uninhabited countryside are examples of this type of occupancy. In urban areas, all spaces are assigned. While some spaces may assume the character of a free occupancy, it is usually for a limited time period (during a festival, for example) or because people ignore the controlling signs (in the case of squatters). These are not true examples of free occupancy, but indications of relaxed or ineffective territorial control.

The Caverns as Free Occupancy

We leave our car on the road, and carrying our gear and equipment, start off on the forty-five minute hike to the caverns. The entrance passage is steep and narrow, and as we proceed it becomes darker, with only intermittent shafts of light penetrating through crevices in the high rock ceiling.

Suddenly we emerge into a large cavern and in the sudden flare of the lights, which are lit by our guide, we find ourselves in a huge hall dominated by intricate rock formations that tower up into the darkness, a darkness that our torches can only dimly penetrate. In the center of the hall is a small pool that is filled with salt water. This is the pool, mentioned in the old manuscripts, in which the God of the Earth was said to have bathed. We go through cavern after cavern, sometimes having to force our way through narrow passages. Our guide has been there several times before, and he alerts us to sudden drops, leads us along level surfaces, provides rope ladders, and tells us of the underground rivers that once, long ago, rushed through these very halls. Suddenly we realize that we are lost and it is a terrifying experience. But then one of our party recognizes a strangely shaped column that we had passed on the way in.

Eventually we return to the dazzling light of day and the caverns are returned to darkness. Back at the car, we open a pack of beer.

The conventions associated with occupancy, as is the case of those associated with play, establish ranges of acceptable site features and user behaviors. Improvement in either area—physical or behavioral—is, then, an appropriate way to improve a setting, and the effectiveness of a change in one depends in part on its compatibility with the other. The conventions govern permanent features of the environment as well as changeable ones, and changes generated by everyday users as well as professional designers. This means that if we as designers create the conditions for the operation of a particular convention, we trigger user-generated changes that are generally appropriate to the setting. In this way we can generate predictable changes in the environment without actually making all the changes ourselves. We can design so that users make a major contribution to the appearance of the environment, giving it a diversity that is quite different from the variety-within-unity that characterizes the work of professional designers, and is more vital, immediate, and meaningful. But to achieve this diversity we must be prepared to give up some control over the form of the environment, and accept user-generated changes as legitimate design decisions, whether or not they satisfy the accepted canons of good taste.

User-generated features in the environment are important not only because of what they do to overall appearance, but because the act of making changes (rather than the changes themselves) gives users a sense of control and responsibility. Taking charge of the physical environment generates a sense of competency and effectiveness, which can be especially useful in community development. For designers this suggests a shift in emphasis from final product to process, or as Korten (1980) describes it, from a blueprint approach to a social learning approach. Korten argues that in community development the first order of priority should be to create not a product, but an organization that is able to formulate, test, reject, and fine-tune programs to suit local conditions and changing circumstances. He describes the social learning approach as a slow process, one that has a high risk of failure and that recognizes the uncertainties and ambiguities inherent in social change. The emphasis must be on central facilitation rather than central control, repeated performance monitoring and self-correction rather than preplanning and final evaluation. The role of the professional should be one that favors

disciplined observation, guided interviews, and informant panels over formal surveys; timeliness over rigor; oral over written communication; informed interpretation over statistical analysis; narrative over numerical presentation; and attention to process and intermediate outcomes as a basis for rapid adaptation over detailed assessment of "final" outcomes. (p. 501)

As professional planners and designers we have two roles: we are experts, acting on behalf of other people and coming up with solutions to their problems; and we are facilitators, helping other people to define and resolve their problems for themselves. In the past we saw ourselves primarily as experts—artists or scientists—and our primary efforts at facilitation were directed at helping clients to appreciate our point of view. But we are increasingly being involved in situations where attempts to play the expert are viewed as intrusive, impertinent, and fuel for opposition, and some of us have come to think of ourselves mainly as facilitators (Howe, 1980). We experiment with new techniques and procedures for including future users in the design process (see, for example, Hatch, 1984; Francis, Cashdan, and Paxson, 1984) and for communicating design information to non-designers (see, for example, Sanoff, 1978; Appleyard and Craik, 1974). We look to the social sciences for ways to make research more responsive to community needs (see, for example, Sommer, 1984; Chavis, Stucky, and Wandersman, 1983). The effect has been to broaden the range of what it is that we do, but it has also led us into new fields, where our role is not defined by custom, we are called upon to do things that we are not trained for, traditional design theories offer little understanding, and the professional culture holds few models.

NOTES

1. Roger Barker (1978 and elsewhere) defines the main characteristics of a behavior setting as:

A pattern of activity bounded in space and time.
The pattern of activity is stable and characteristic.
A behavior setting contains a mix of human and physical components that are mutually dependent.
It is not dependent on particular people, nor are people dependent upon a particular setting.
There are mechanisms to maintain conformity to the overall pattern.

2. The study was conducted by the Baltimore City Department of Planning, assisted by a grant from the National Endowment for the Arts through the City Options Program. Information was obtained from permit applications, observations at 25 festivals, interviews with 425 festival-goers at these festivals, mail questionnaires received from organizers of 64 festivals, and in-depth interviews with 10 organizers. For the complete findings of the study, see Baltimore City Department of Planning (1977).

3. Fully 95 percent of the organizers felt that their festival had accomplished their particular purpose, 65 percent had held the event before, and 89 percent planned to hold it again the following year, most of them in the same location; 30 percent of festival-goers interviewed had been to the same festival on a previous occasion.

4. A number of studies have found that while children were out playing, many of them were not playing in the playgrounds provided for them. See, for example, Ward, 1978; Brower, 1977a; Gold, 1977; Cooper, 1975; Department of the Environment, 1973; and Allen, 1968.

5. The booth that the city supplied for festivals was a standard, rather primitive, makeshift affair that was manufactured, delivered, and assembled by staff of the Bureau of Special Services. We asked community groups and city agencies about the good and bad features of this booth, and it was suggested that the provisions for display, enclosure, attachment, electric power, and decoration be improved. We then designed a system of modular components to replace the standard booth. The components could be assembled and arranged in a variety of ways to suit different kinds of uses. A prototype was built and put to use at several festivals. The new booths were sturdier than the old ones and more obviously an expression of design intent, but in an environment where the temporary and the makeshift were the order of the day, these qualities turned out to be not all that important. Add to this the fact that the new elements were heavier to transport and more expensive to repair and we can see why the new design never caught on.

6. This example incorporates material developed in two earlier papers (Brower 1980 and 1965).

6

A Home in the Wilderness

When residents feel threatened, a safe environment looks very attractive.

In a lithograph titled *My Cottage Home,* published in 1866 (Simkin, 1955), Currier and Ives presented a popular image of the ideal home (see Photograph 11). The picture shows a pretty, colonial style cottage with many windows, standing in a pleasant, fertile, and civilized countryside. The land immediately around the house has been appropriated, ordered, and domesticated; planted, fenced, and furnished. The cottage and garden show a concern for appearances that goes well beyond practical necessity: the building features are arranged to conform to stylistic practices, service uses are placed where they cannot be seen from the road, the front yard is landscaped for pleasure rather than work, and it provides an attractive setting for the house.

Many of the elements in the picture are nostalgic and outdated, but the overall image of home as a pavilion in a garden, a place that celebrates the connection of people with their physical environment, retains its popular appeal. It dominates contemporary design literature, where it finds its purest expression in descriptions of traditional Japanese domestic architecture:

[T]he ideal abode is associated above all with the blossoms of spring, the evening cool of summer, the bright moonlight of autumn, and the hushed snowfall of winter. (Ashihara, 1983, p. 6)

This image of home is predicated on the assumption that the environment is hospitable and friendly, and that residents are safe to relax, open themselves to it, and enjoy it.

11 My Cottage Home

In a hospitable environment the house opens itself up to its surroundings.

But there is another image of home, and this, too, was represented by Currier and Ives, in a print issued four years later and called *A Home in the Wilderness* (see Photograph 12). The picture shows a cold, lonely, unknown, and untamed countryside. In a forest clearing, under heavy cover of snow, stands a crude log cabin. It has strong walls, a stout door, and small windows. Smoke rises from the chimney. The cabin is a place of refuge in a hostile environment; it offers warmth, protection, and nurture—escape from the harsh realities of life out of doors. It is built to satisfy basic shelter needs in the most practical and efficient way, using materials at hand and eschewing frivolity. Logs are piled up near the doorway, and there is no attempt to improve the land around the cabin.

It is reasonable to assume that given the choice, people prefer to live in a friendly environment rather than a hostile one, and so given the choice, that they prefer a cottage in the country to a cabin in the wilderness. But if people, through choice or circumstances, *were* to find themselves in the wilderness, they would opt for a cabin rather than a cottage because the cabin is better suited to life in a hostile environment. This chapter is about high-threat residential areas—a contemporary counterpart of the wilderness. I will try to show that in high-threat residential areas, residents' image of home is that of a cabin in the wilderness (not a cottage in the country), and that this image has important implications for the way people see and use the near-home environment.

High-threat environments are those that, in the eyes of their residents, are plagued with problems and dangers. Residents are afraid of bodily harm (assault and automobile traffic), loss of property (burglary and vandalism), loss of health (lead paint and rats), and threats to their social and psychological well-being (verbal hostility, exploitation, intimidation, eviction; being ignored, defied, abused, or intruded upon). They feel threatened by challenges, real or imagined, to their values, their ideas about the way things should be done. They are suspicious of features of the environment that are at all unusual,[1] and feel threatened by changes whose consequences are unpredictable and over which they have no control (Winkel, 1981).

Fears and problems in high-threat areas are expressed in uncivil, irresponsible, and inconsiderate behavior, including damage to the physical environment through intent or neglect. The level of threat is highest when it comes from within—from fellow residents rather than outsiders—and it can be measured by crime statistics, police calls for assistance, arguments and fights among neighbors, automobile accidents, the number of people who are drunk and on drugs. A study in several high-threat areas in Baltimore (Brower, 1977a) showed that residents were fearful for themselves, their family, property, and possessions. Some residents did not like to carry wallets or pocketbooks when they went out, and they went out of their way to avoid certain streets. Many did not like to leave their home, especially at night, and they only really felt safe inside their own house or in the house of a friend. They were suspicious of outsiders and mistrustful of one another. One resident was convinced that children in the playground were just waiting for an opportunity to rob her.

A HOME IN THE WILDERNESS.

12   A Home in the Wilderness

In a hostile environment the house closes itself off from its surroundings.

[Y]ou've got children from every place; from all around. They're destructive. There are people around that I have never seen before. Who plays basketball at eleven o'clock, twelve o'clock, one o'clock in the morning, ten o'clock at night? You don't play basketball all night! That's a gag. And the ball come into your yard—that's a gag to see if you're home. See, that's a gag.

Residents' perceptions of threat stem from personal experiences and firsthand accounts, as well as from hearsay, and the general "climate of fear" that is pervasive in high-threat residential areas. Some people feel threatened in an environment where others do not, because they are more vulnerable, or because they feel that they have more to lose. For example, women tend to feel more threatened than men, elderly people feel more threatened than non-elderly, parents are more fearful for their children, and husbands are more fearful for their wives than they are for themselves. Children are fearful of things, real as well as imagined, that adults are only dimly aware of. Studies have also shown that because educated people tend to have higher expectations, they perceive problems where less well educated people do not. People who have lived in the area for a longer period of time, compared with newcomers, tend to see some things as more of a problem ("Things were better in the old days") and other things as less of a problem ("We have learned to live with it"). Certain physical and social characteristics of residential areas increase the likelihood of threatening conditions (these include higher density, the inclusion of non-residential uses, through traffic, unemployment, low income, high percentage of renters, high percentage of teenagers), but in the end, people's perception of threat is subjective and does not necessarily correspond with objective circumstances.[2]

Living with threat affects the way people see their environment and the way they behave in it.[3] A common reaction to threat is to redraw the mental boundaries of one's home space so as to exclude the source of the threat; that is, people shrink the size of the area that they think of as home until the amount of threat it contains is reduced to manageable size. Because of the subjective nature of the boundaries of the home space, some residents think of an entire neighborhood as home (so that it includes house, yards, sidewalks, alleys, playgrounds, small parks, and local stores); while for others, home space is reduced to one street, or a single house or apartment. A smaller home space usually means a more threatening environment. Hunter (1974) found that when residents of a white neighborhood were faced with black in-migration, they redefined the area of their community so as to exclude the black population (p. 141). Taylor et al. (1980, pp. 8.30–32) found that residents who were more fearful of their physical environment had a smaller area that they called home.[4] Appleyard (1981) found that when residents were faced with the danger of increased traffic on their street, they shrank the area that they called home. Elderly residents, who are generally more fearful than the non-elderly, perceived a smaller home space. There is also a connection between the perceived extent of home and feelings of responsibility: renters felt less responsibility for the physical environment than owners, and they recognized a smaller home space.

Shrinking the home space has important implications for behavior. Studies have shown that as one's subjective estimate of distance from a place increases, one's emotional involvement with the place, that is, the degree to which one really cares about what happens there, falls off very steeply (Gould and White, 1974, p. 41). Home is the one place of all places where people feel the greatest responsibility for the way the physical environment looks and is used (Taylor et al., 1981a). When one mentally transfers a part of the residential environment from home to non-home, one is psychologically distancing oneself from the place and transferring it out of one's sphere of primary responsibility. One feels safer because while the threat has not been eliminated, it is now someone else's problem. In one interview a resident told Taylor et al. about several murders that had taken place on the next block, but she rated her own neighborhood as safe; she simply excluded the next block in her definition of her neighborhood. Some residents drew the boundaries even smaller. One gave her block the best possible ratings on a number of problem and fear scales; and then, in conversation, she said,

I don't hear nothin'. I don't see nothin'. I don't know nothin' going on. I wouldn't interfere with anythin' anywhere. Next thing you'll find yourself dead in an alley. (Brower et al., 1984, p. 210)

This resident had drawn her home space so as to exclude everything outside her house. Her perceptions were reflected in her behavior: she stayed close to home and at the slightest hint of trouble she simply went in and closed the door.

In high-threat environments, therefore, the area that residents associate with home, and over which they are prepared to exercise the responsibilities associated with home, is likely to be very small. It may not extend beyond a city block, and in many instances it will be far smaller than that. This has important implications for resident participation in the planning, design, and management of neighborhood facilities: it means that one can only really count on the interest and commitment of residents who live in the immediate vicinity of the site. By way of comparison, residents in low-threat neighborhoods perceive their home as extending farther into the environment (Taylor et al. 1981a).

Not all residents will withdraw in the face of threat. Some will define the threat as a temporary problem in their home space and instead of pulling back, they will join with other residents and mobilize to reestablish and strengthen their boundaries. Unfortunately, this kind of collective action is difficult to bring about in high-threat areas, where people tend to keep to themselves, and mistrust and fear dominate their relationships with one another. This is due, in part, to the perceived heterogeneity of the population.

People generally like to live with others of the same kind as themselves, and as a result desirable residential areas tend to exhibit a certain degree of homogeneity. High-threat areas tend to be less homogeneous than low-threat areas; that is, residents in high-threat areas are more likely to see their neighbors as incompatible types of people (Taylor et al., 1981a). We do not know just what it is that makes people feel that their neighbors are not the same kind of people as themselves. It does not seem to be based on objective measures such as differences in age and length of residence, education and prestige of employment, income, household size, or marital status. It does not even seem to be based on *perceptions* that their neighbors are different in age, religion, income, or education (Taylor et al., 1981). Instead, it seems to be a global judgment based on such things as childrearing practices, respectability, responsibility, privacy, property maintenance, and civil behavior.[5]

While the concept of incompatibility challenges analysts, its effects are easy to recognize: residents in high-threat neighborhoods tend to know fewer people in the neighborhood, have fewer friends on the block, and are less willing to work together (Taylor et al., 1981a).

As part of a study in a city block in a high-threat neighborhood (Brower et al., 1976), we tried to assist residents to form a community organization in order to work on common problems. In an effort to increase communication, a biweekly block newspaper was introduced and residents were invited to submit stories, opinions, notices, personal histories, and advertisements. But the paper did not last long because—it soon became clear—the general philosophy among residents was that it was safest to keep to oneself, that to become too conspicuous was to present a clear target, and that to take sides on a public issue was to invite reprisal.

We tried a new tack. In order to persuade residents to look at the block as a social unit with opportunities for mutual assistance, we hired two local teenage girls and let it be known that for a nominal fee (all income to go to the block association) the girls would be available to assist individual householders with chores such as cleaning, moving, carrying, and doing odd jobs. A number of elderly residents lived on the block, and we thought that they would welcome this kind of assistance. But there were no takers. The reason, we discovered, was that residents felt that if the girls saw what possessions they had, the girls would steal something, or they would tell their boyfriends who would first break in and then steal something. Residents were unwilling to allow strangers into their homes.

Because of the prevailing air of mistrust, community organizations in high-threat neighborhoods tend to represent only certain groups or interests (for example, homeowners and not renters) and they are fragile, and often depend on the leadership of a strong individual or the sponsorship of an outside organization. The most successful form of community organization in high-threat areas is exemplified by the churches and social clubs; these are true community occupancies, with homogeneous membership, and with built-in mechanisms for initiating new members, screening out undesirables, and maintaining established standards of behavior. This suggests that community facilities are more likely to be properly managed by such restricted groups than by associations whose membership is open to all. There are many examples of facilities in high-threat areas, including streets (Newman, 1980) and parks (Francis, Cashdan, and Paxson, 1984), that have been successfully managed by private resident organizations. It is important that the organization be given full authority to regulate access to and use of their facility. The facility itself should be visually identified with the managing group and it should be provided with physical barriers, and clearly demarcated entry points that can be closed off. The managing group may well decide to make the facility accessible to all, but that should be their decision, and it should be clear to the public that permission to use the facility can be withdrawn in the event of unacceptable behavior.

This is not to say that open resident associations cannot work in high-threat areas but to form them and to sustain them requires considerable effort. They will not develop automatically. It is important, then, for designers to be concerned about the management of spaces in the near-home environment. Management is not usually an issue in low-threat areas because informal social mechanisms are capable of protecting desired uses against incompatible ones. But in high-threat areas, not only do residents have weaker feelings of responsibility and control (Taylor et al., 1981a), but in addition, the social mechanisms for exercising control are far less effective. Management creates the context within which a space will be used, and so user satisfaction may depend more upon the design of the management system than of the physical elements. Consequently, management is a legitimate design concern.

One of the prime concerns of all managers is to protect their space against intrusion by outsiders. This either means erecting physical obstructions that will prevent outsiders from coming in (barriers), or displaying notices that warn outsiders to stay out (signs). Barriers include walls, fences, gates, locks, shutters, bars, chains, and dogs. Signs include written notices such as "Private Property" and "Trespassers Will Be Prosecuted"; but they also include the display of household objects (such as flowerboxes, curtains, lawns, and ceramic cats) that signify that the house is occupied and that because they are associated with and reflect the presence of the occupant of the house, are seen as proxies for the physical presence of the person him- or herself.[6] People tend to equate signs of occupancy with safety; they are more fearful in areas where there are vacant buildings, peeling paint, and trash.[7]

In a study of Baltimore neighborhoods (Brower, Dockett, and Taylor, 1983),

Figure 6.1   Drawings of Backyards

The sixteen drawings show all possible combinations of four variables: boundary fence/no fence, boundary curb/no curb, display of ornaments/no ornaments, and planting/no planting. A companion set of drawings, identical in all respects except that the person on the chair was omitted, was shown to a different subset of participants. Illustration courtesy of Baltimore City Department of Planning.

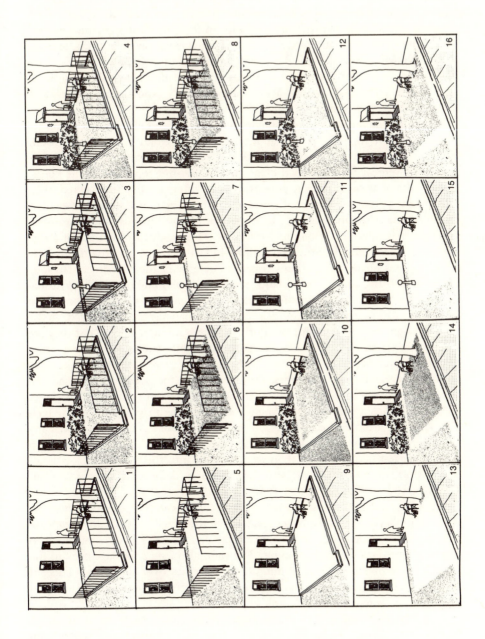

a sample of forty residents, split between high-threat and low-threat areas, were shown sixteen line drawings of a residential back yard (see Figure 6.1). Each drawing included or omitted one or more of four different signs and barriers (boundary curb, boundary fence, display of ornaments, and planting), and the sixteen drawings represented all possible combinations of these features. Each participant examined the set of drawings and then rated each drawing in response to a series of questions about safety, privacy, and trespass. The study resulted in the following conclusions.

In low-threat areas, where residents live in a more civil society, signs are usually enough to deter potential intruders (other than animals and young children who have not been enculturated), and so manicured lawns and well tended flowerbeds will, in effect, create an outsider-free zone around the house. In high-threat areas, however, proxies will not automatically be accepted: their validity and potency will be challenged and tested. Lawns and flowerbeds will be trampled unless the intruders are kept away by physical means, and unless they perceive that there is a good chance they will be caught. In high-threat areas, therefore, there must be an emphasis on physical barriers, and the addition of warning signs further strengthens residents' defense of their territory. (In low-threat areas, this kind of redundancy serves no useful purpose.) All territorial claims must be proclaimed loudly and defended aggressively, and residents must be prepared to intervene the moment their occupancies are challenged.

Some signs are more potent than others. Signs are more effective if they are closely associated with the identity of the occupant; that is, if they represent personal preferences and affiliations. Signs are also more effective if, like good maintenance and embellishments, they imply that the occupant has made an investment in the physical environment and cares about what happens there. Temporary signs are often more potent than permanent signs because one feels that they are a more direct reflection of the occupant.[8] The sight of washing hung out to dry, a sprinkler going on the lawn, an open window, a rose bush in bloom, suggest more strongly than features built into the architecture or landscape, that the resident is present, cares, and is likely to be on the lookout (Brower et al., 1983; Rapoport, 1982).

Signs have different messages for different audiences. To potential offenders they mean "Keep Out". To other residents of the neighborhood, they indicate that the householder is responsible, respectable, a good neighbor, someone who can be counted on for civil behavior. The signs also send a message back to the householders themselves, confirming their authority over the space. This, in turn, emboldens them: residents are more likely to intervene to defend a fenced yard than an unfenced one (Brower et al., 1983).

It is especially important, then, when we design in high-threat areas, to incorporate a variety of barriers and signs that distinguish private spaces from public spaces and from one another, and to protect them against intrusion.[9] Because user-generated signs are so effective, we must provide the proper facilities and management conditions so that residents are encouraged to personalize, improve, and maintain their home and near-home spaces (Brower et al., 1976).

We must do this even if it means sacrificing the visual integrity and unity of our overall design. Of course, the best defense of all is the physical presence of the residents themselves, and so every attempt should be made to ensure that near-home spaces are actively used.

The use of near-home spaces raises another set of considerations. The concepts of privacy and seclusion as applied to the near-home environment are interpreted quite differently in high-threat and low-threat residential environments. In low-threat environments, these are highly desirable qualities, suggestive of relaxation and peacefulness. In high-threat neighborhoods, people are afraid to be out alone. They avoid solitary outdoor places where they cannot be seen, and prefer spaces that are open to view and where there are other people around to see them.[10] This is one of the reasons for the popularity of the streetfront.

There is a temptation for planners and designers to use the safety-in-numbers rationale as an argument for increasing pedestrian activity in all neighborhood spaces; but this may be faulty reasoning. In one study in a high-threat, row house neighborhood (Brower, 1977b), residents were shown eight models of alternative block layouts. Each model showed a block of rowhouses, but each included different combinations of streetfront and innerblock spaces, and of through-access and dead-end spaces. Participants were asked to select the safest block and to give reasons for their choice. Most decisions involved through-access-streetfronts and dead-end-inner-block spaces. Selections revealed a common underlying rationale about what made a space safe and what made it unsafe. This was differently interpreted, depending upon participants' assumptions about the way the spaces would be used. (See Photographs 13 and 14.)

For some, the streetfront was the safest place because it was open, nothing was hidden, and it was actively used by neighboring residents; this meant that if you should get into trouble there would be people to see and help. For others, the streetfront was the most dangerous place because there were so many outsiders who could not be trusted. Some felt that the inner-block dead-end spaces were the safest because there was no reason for outsiders to be there, and so they would be used by residents only. Others felt that these same spaces were the most dangerous, because if outsiders came in they were less likely to be observed, and if you were trapped there was no way to escape. What this adds up to is that residents felt safest in spaces that were actively used by other residents; that is, people whom they knew and whom they could rely on in case of need. They felt least safe in spaces that were mainly used by outsiders.[11]

In another study (Taylor et al., 1976), block residents were shown a series of pictures of a block facade; some of the pictures showed residents sitting out and others did not (see Figure 6.2). Again, participants were asked to nominate the safest block. Results showed that blocks with residents sitting out were considered far safer than blocks without. The visible presence of neighbors was clearly a safety feature. One of the reasons people recreated on the streetfront, then, was that they felt safer there; and the fact that they recreated there contributed to the feeling of safety. There was, however, a price to pay: blocks with people

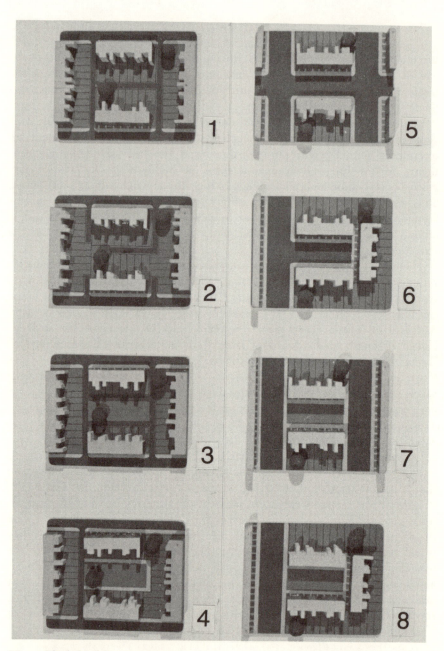

13   Block Models

The eight block models show all possible combinations of three variables: houses face or back up against one another, are separated by a path (street or alley) or a park, and the path or park allows through access or it is a dead end. Model 5 (front, path, through) was rated both as the most safe and the least safe block; its opposite counterparts were block 2 (back, path, dead end) and block 4 (back, park, dead end). Photograph courtesy of Baltimore City Department of Planning.

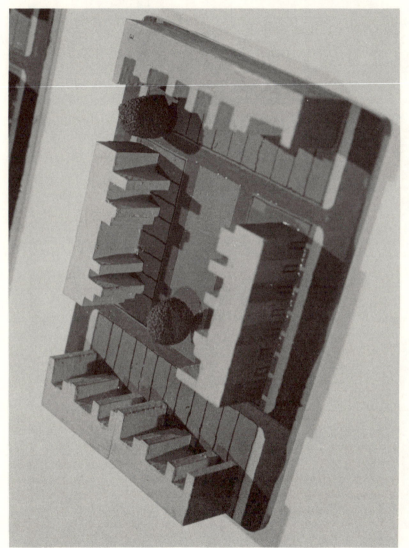

14 Block Model 3

Block model 3 shows houses backing up to one another, around an inner-block park with pedestrian through-access. Photograph courtesy of Baltimore City Department of Planning.

Figure 6.2   Drawings of Block Facades

The eight drawings show all possible combinations of three variables: people sitting out/no people, display of curtains and flowers/no display, color differentiation of facades/no color differentiation. Illustration courtesy of Baltimore City Department of Planning.

sitting out were also identified as the ones where people were least likely to mind their own business, and as the ones that were most likely to be littered.

In the study using block models, described earlier, participants were asked to identify the best places for children to play. The responses showed that in the inner-block spaces children would be protected from the automobile, but they could not be well supervised and so they were at risk from anti-social elements; on the streetfront the children would be under constant surveillance and could be protected from anti-social elements, but they were exposed to the dangers of the traffic. Participants found this a hard choice to make. In reality though, when given a choice between the streetfront and inner-block spaces, most children played on the street. Social elements were apparently more threatening than automobile traffic (Brower, 1977a).

I have tried to show that residents in high-threat areas tend to see home as a refuge in a hostile environment, and that this viewpoint is expressed in the way they feel about the environment and the way that they use it. Architects and planners working in these areas, who approach the design of near-home spaces with a cottage-in-the-country image, are unlikely to see things as residents do, and may unwittingly contribute to making the areas more dangerous and less livable. Designing a prosthetic environment does not eliminate the causes of threat, but it makes threat easier to cope with.

NOTES

1. When rating a number of visual qualities for their contribution toward making a place attractive to live in, residents in a high-threat neighborhood placed a very low value on the quality "unusual" because, they reasoned, when something is unusual it is unpredictable and potentially dangerous (Baltimore City Department of Planning, 1973).

2. There has been a good deal of research on the environmental factors that contribute to fear. For a review of this research, see Heinzelmann, 1981, and DeBow, McCabe, and Kaplan, 1979.

3. A central issue in any discussion of high-threat environments is whether to eliminate the causes of threat or whether to make threat easier to live with. The question has been debated for many years (see, for example, Rainwater, 1966, with following comment by Montgomery). I take the position that threatening environments are not acceptable; that social and economic reforms are the main avenues for removing the causes of the problem, but these will take a long time and in the meantime we cannot ignore the fact that high-threat environments exist, and that people have to live in them. They create a special context for design.

4. This paper draws extensively from the findings of a study by Taylor, Gottfredson, and Brower (1980, 1981a) of informal social controls in residential areas in Baltimore. These findings were further developed in Taylor and Brower, 1985; Brower et al., 1984, 1983; Taylor et al., 1984, 1981b.

5. Gans (1968) writes of residential homogeneity:

Little is known about what characteristics must be shared before people feel themselves to be compatible with others. We do not know for certain if they must have common backgrounds, or similar interests, or shared values, or combinations of these. Social relations are based, not on census data, but on subjectively experienced definitions of homogeneity and heterogeneity which terminate in judgments of compatibility or incompatibility. (p. 156)

Rapoport (1977, esp. pp. 249–265) notes that clustering in homogenous residential areas serves to reduce threat:

People like to live with others who belong to the same culture: share values, ideas and norms; understand and respond to the same symbols, agree about child rearing, interaction, density and lifestyle—and hence leisure, food, clothing style, manners and rules. . . . By having clear, fixed and recognized areas, boundaries, rules, relationships, social hierarchies, physical devices, space organization, appropriate cues, symbols and markers, there are fewer problems and stress is reduced. . . . The result is that predictability is increased (or unpredictability reduced), with clear effects on perceived density, crowding, overload and stress. . . . (pp. 256–257)

Lofland (1973) describes how people use homogeneous areas as the basis for classifying strangers: the neighborhood they live in tells one something about the kind of people they are. Spatial classification of this kind makes it easier for people to cope in a heterogeneous society.

6. I use the word "signs" to mean all forms of symbolic representation, whether intentional of unintentional, that are interpreted to mean appropriation or territorial possession, including those sometimes referred to as markers, signals, symbols, traces, and cues. For distinctions between different types of signs, see Rapoport, 1982. For a discussion of the form and function of signs in the residential environment, see Appleyard, 1979.

7. A study by Lewis and Maxfield (1980) showed that residents' perceptions of crime are shaped not so much by the neighborhood conditions reflected in the crime statistics as by the level of incivility in their community. Indicators of incivility include abandoned buildings, vandalism, and trash. Earlier, Hunter (1978) referred to these as "symbols of incivility".

In a study by Taylor, Gottfredson, and Brower (1980), 32 slides of individual houses in Baltimore (most of them row houses) were selected to represent varying conditions of care. Each house was rated for the level of gardening, ornament, cleanliness, and structural repair. The slides were shown to twelve city planners. They were asked to rate each house in relation to nine statements about neighborhood safety. The correlations of the SAFETY ratings and CARE ratings are shown on page 91 (all correlations significant to p < 0.05). A higher care rating was correlated with a better, safer neighborhood. The procedure was repeated with fifteen graduate students, and produced similar results.

8. In low income neighborhoods with a high percentage of renters, building improvements are not seen as the responsibility of the occupant; they reflect instead upon the landlord.

9. These ideas are explored in some detail in the "defensible space" literature, especially Newman (1973) and reviews by DuBow, McCabe, and Kaplan (1979) and Heinzelmann (1981). Also see Heinig and Maxfield (1978).

10. Heinzelmann (1981) notes that opportunities for concealment are linked to offender behavior (that is, the choice of targets), fear of crime, and occurrence of crime (p. 91).

11. Baumer and Hunter (1979) found that residents who perceived more pedestrian traffic on their street were also more fearful of crime, and those residents who had weak ties to their neighbors were more fearful of pedestrian traffic than those with strong ties. This is explained in part by the fact that the latter felt they could call on a neighbor in time of need.

SAFETY	CARE			
	Gardening	Ornaments	Clean	Repair
1. If you went into the space you'd have the feeling you were on someone else's property	0.44	0.37	0.46	0.65
2. The people who live here take care of the space.	0.69		0.59	0.73
3. This is a low income neighborhood.	- 0.68		- 0.60	- 0.66
4. If you should go into the space, the resident is likely to notice.	0.58		0.50	0.67
5. If you should go into the space, the resident is likely to watch you.	0.53	0.34	0.56	0.70
6. This is a safe neighborhood.	0.70		0.63	0.70
7. You would be nervous about being in the space alone at night if you lived here.	- 0.71	- 0.30	- 0.55	- 0.64
8. Something left out in the space is an easy target for a burglar.				- 0.46
9. If you should go into the space, a neighbor is likely to watch you.	0.45	0.50	0.40	0.61

Part II

7

Introduction

Case studies give a resident's-eye-view of a Baltimore neighborhood and the findings have implications for design.

I have argued that in order to represent the design concerns of residents one has to look at the environment from a resident's point of view. The following chapters will illustrate the design implications of such an approach, using case studies from Baltimore.

All of these case studies were done in a low-income, black, inner-city neighborhood known as Harlem Park. At the time the studies began there was public concern about living conditions in low-income inner-city areas and there were public programs to fund improvements. A number of parks had been built in Harlem Park and the Department of Planning wanted to know whether these parks had improved the housing environment in a significant way, and whether they should be repeated in other neighborhoods. The studies focused on residents' attitudes and behaviors in the parks, compared to other neighborhood open spaces such as streets, sidewalks, alleys, and yards.

The first studies were followed by two rounds of additional studies. There were several reasons why all of these studies were concentrated in Harlem Park. First, the objective was not only to collect information, but also to apply what was learned in the research, and this meant returning to the same neighborhood. Second, the information called for replication because it seemed to contradict some of the assumptions of traditional design training, and so understanding residents' responses in Harlem Park was a way of re-examining basic ideas and values in the design profession.

Harlem Park is not typical of all residential areas. There are residential areas that are unlike Harlem Park in many important respects. But what we found in these case studies is supported by the findings of other studies in the United States and elsewhere, which means that Harlem Park represents a type of residential area, and the findings in Harlem Park apply to other areas of the same type. In addition, as with other case studies, the particular situation serves to illustrate the workings of general principles and, in this case, residents' responses in Harlem Park raise issues that must be considered in the design of all residential environments.

The studies in Harlem Park spanned a period of thirteen years. The first round (1971–1973) included twelve blocks, seven of them with parks; the second round (1974–1977) included twenty-six blocks, fourteen with parks; and the final round (1980–1983) included twelve blocks with parks. Actually, the survey area covered three abutting neighborhoods, all predominantly black and low-income; but as 39 of the 50 study sites were in Harlem Park, and as sites in the other neighborhoods produced similar results, I have found it simpler in this account to ascribe all findings to Harlem Park. The first round of studies also included two sites in an adjacent predominantly white, middle-income neighborhood, and findings from the middle-income sites will be used for purposes of comparison.

The studies included a number of interventions, and some of the interventions did not succeed. Approaches that worked elsewhere did not necessarily work in Harlem Park. This report will dwell on less-than-successful efforts, because they illustrate more vividly than successes the special design problems in Harlem Park. The studies addressed the questions: who used each of the outdoor spaces, for what purposes, in what manner, and how could the conditions of use be improved?

8

Description of the Study Area

Harlem Park is a predominantly black, low-income neighborhood in Baltimore's inner city. In the early 1960s it underwent renewal, during which time the houses were rehabilitated and 29 inner-block parks were built.

Harlem Park was developed around the time of the Civil War to provide housing for middle-income families, and it remained essentially unchanged until the second World War. Then a major change occurred. During the 1940s and 1950s, the white middle-class families left for the newly-developing suburbs and they were replaced by black, low-income households, many of whom had come to Baltimore to work in the wartime industries. The houses were subdivided into rental apartments and the physical condition of the area deteriorated.

In 1959, the City selected Harlem Park for its first significant residential urban renewal project, and between 1960 and 1970 two thousand houses were rehabilitated. Most of these houses were on main streets. There were also small houses on narrow streets that ran through the center of the blocks, but these houses were in bad condition and they had to be demolished. This left about a half-acre parcel of vacant land in the middle of the block, which was then made into a public park. Of the 32 residential blocks in Harlem Park, 29 have inner-block parks. Each park is visible from the backs of houses and can only be seen from the street if one looks up the alley. A typical park has several trees, paving, a patch of grass, and climbing equipment. Residents participated fully in the design of the parks. At the same time, the urban renewal program brought new schools, a recreation center, and a small group of retail stores. Construction

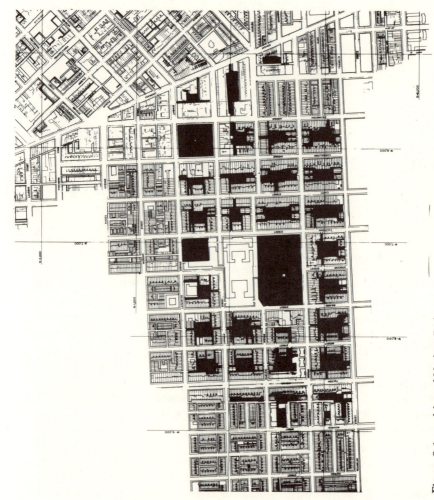

Figure 8.1　　Map of Harlem Park

The map shows the 29 inner-block parks created through the renewal program. Illustration courtesy of Baltimore City Department of Planning.

15 Street Facades in Harlem Park

A composite picture of a typical block face in Harlem Park. The inner-block park is visible through the alley entrance. Photograph courtesy of Baltimore City Department of Planning.

16   Inner-Block Park in Harlem Park

The inner-block parks are paved and they have fixed play equipment. This is one of the more attractive parks because the trees have survived. Photograph courtesy of Baltimore City Department of Planning.

continued slowly through the 1970s, resulting in several new apartment buildings, including two for elderly tenants.

Most of the buildings in Harlem Park are row houses, and they create blocks with continuous street facades, marked by a succession of stone or wooden steps, and interrupted by narrow alley entranceways. The alleys run behind the houses; they are used to store trash (although some blocks have collections from the sidewalk); some are used for oil delivery and by repair crews attending to utilities. Each house has a fenced-in backyard with a gate onto the alley. The houses themselves vary in height from two to four floors. The fronts are of brick, most of them of simple design, which have evolved over the years into a mosaic of reds and browns interspersed with grey formstone. Many of the larger houses, and most of those in the poorer section of the neighborhood, have been divided into apartments. There is considerable variation in the condition of the interiors, and furnishings vary from comfortable to minimal, and from tasteful to makeshift.

Harlem Park has a wide range of scattered non-residential uses. These include churches, small "mom and pop" food stores, clubs, bars, and cut-rate liquor outlets. The professional services include doctors, lawyers, hairdressers, beauticians, notaries, undertakers, pharmacists, tax consultants, and real estate agents; and there are places for cleaning and repairing clothes and automobiles. A number of unofficial businesses operate out of basements, and in the hot summer months some of them spill out onto the sidewalks; these include printing, repairing appliances, upholstering, and selling candy and a crushed-ice-and-syrup confection popularly known as snowballs. Hawkers with horse-drawn carts (popularly known as street a-rabs) are a familiar sight in the streets of Harlem Park.

Sociologically, Harlem Park is typical of many other low-income, inner-city neighborhoods. When the study began in 1971, there were, according to the U.S. census, just under 10,000 people living in Harlem Park; 99.7 percent were black (46 percent for the city as a whole) and 81 percent were renters (58 percent for the city). The average estimated market value of owner-occupied homes was about $6,500 ($11,500 for the city), 26 percent of households had female heads (16 percent for the city), and 14 percent of the housing units had more than one person per room (9 percent for the city). The crime rate was high and most residents agreed that it was a serious problem. They also complained about drugs, trash, and noise. Unemployment was high, and there were many children. Community-wide organizations were fragmented and ineffective. Residents were mistrustful of their neighbors and of city government. Residential mobility was high, but there were also many stable, long-term residents, who felt that things had been better in the past.

9

Casebook

A selection of the findings in Harlem Park is presented in order to give a feeling for the living conditions in the neighborhood. The complete findings of these studies are available elsewhere (see, for example, Brower, 1986, 1977a, 1977b; Brower, Dockett, and Taylor, 1983; Brower, Gray, and Stough, 1977, 1976; Gray and Brower, 1977; Brower and Williamson, 1974; Baltimore City Department of Planning, 1973, 1972, 1971). The methods used to collect information included interviews with residents, observations, person counts, doll-play games with children, and interventions.

WHERE THE PEOPLE WERE

Walking Census

For twelve weeks during the summer, a systematic count was made of people who were out-of-doors in twenty-four selected blocks in Harlem Park. Twelve of these blocks had inner-block parks and twelve had no parks. The count was repeated on four days each week, and on each observation day it was repeated in the early afternoon (approximately 1:30 p.m.) and in the evening (approximately 5:00 p.m.). At each count, census takers walked around and through each block and observed streets, sidewalks, steps, porches, yards, alleys, and parks. People were classified by age group, sex, location, and activity. In subsequent analyses, these activities were classified either as *recreational* or *non-recreational*. Recreational uses included playing, roller skating, playing ball, talking, sitting, playing on equipment, and gardening. Where appropriate, activity cate-

Table 9.1   Walking Census: Number of People Observed Out of Doors, by Activity by Block Type (Average number of people per census)

	Park block	Non-park block
People recreating	38.5 (79%)	24.8 (78%)
People not recreating	10.4 (21%)	6.9 (22%)
Total	48.9 (100%)	31.7 (100%)

gories were combined (like sitting and talking, running and playing) and the combined activities were counted as recreational if one of the components was recreational. Non-recreational activities included walking, standing, running, cleaning, and working (for example, mail carriers and street hawkers).

In all, over 40,000 people were observed, an average of about 49 persons per census per park block and 32 persons per each non-park block. Children made up about half of this population. Of the remaining half, about two-thirds were adults and one-third were teenagers. There were more males than females.

The census showed that:

There were more people out-of-doors in park blocks than in non-park blocks, but about the same percentage of people in park and non-park blocks were recreating (Table 9.1).

There were very few recreators in the rear yards. Most recreators were on the streetfront. This was true whether or not there was a park in the block. Blocks with parks had more recreators on the streetfront than in the parks, and recreators on the streetfront outnumbered pedestrians. This was true of all age/sex groups and at all times of day. (See Figs. 9.1, 9.2.)

There was a different composition of recreators on the streetfront and in the inner-block parks: the parks contained a disproportionately high percentage of children and teenage boys, and a disproportionately low percentage of adults. (See Table 9.2.)

The number of recreators increased in the late afternoon, both on the streetfront and in the inner-block parks. This was true for all age/sex groups. The proportion of teenage boys in the parks increased. (See Table 9.3.)

Driving Census

The route of the driving census included 270 block faces in three neighborhoods. Two of the neighborhoods were black and low-income, while the third was white, middle- and upper-middle income. Counts were made from a car moving slowly along a preassigned route, and census takers counted all the people who were visible in parks (eight neighborhood parks were included on the census route), and on porches, steps, and sidewalks. There were virtually no frontyards in the study area, and few inner-block spaces were visible from the

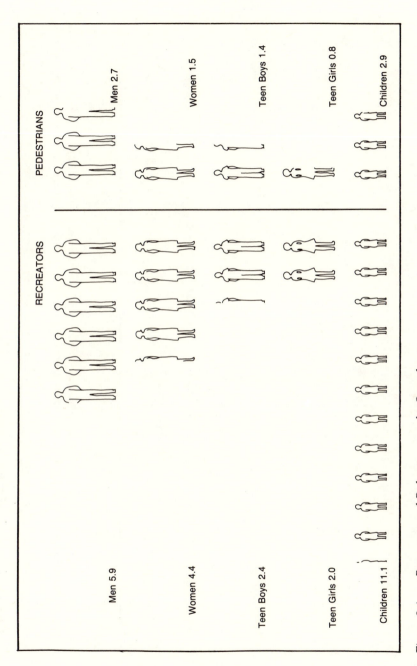

Figure 9.1   Recreators and Pedestrians on the Streetfront

The illustration shows, for an average census, the number and activity of people who were on the streetfront in a typical block with an inner-block park. Most people in each age/sex group were using the streetfront for recreational purposes. Recreation was a major function of the streetfront. Illustration courtesy of Baltimore City Department of Planning.

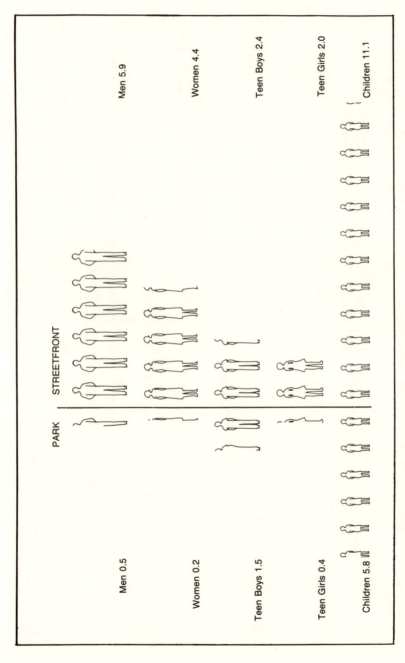

Figure 9.2 Recreators on the Streetfront and in the Park

The illustration shows for a typical block with an inner-block park, the number, location, and composition of people who were recreating at the time of an average census. More people in each age/sex group were recreating on the streetfront than in the park. Children represented the largest single group of users both on the streetfront and in the park. The parks had proportionately fewer adults and more teenage boys, which helps to explain why children experienced more problems there. Illustration courtesy of Baltimore City Department of Planning.

Table 9.2   Walking Census: People Recreating in an Average Park Block, by Location within Block, by Age/Sex Groupings (Average number of people per census)

Location	Men	Women	Teen Boys	Teen Girls	Children	All People
Streetfront	5.9	4.4	2.4	2.0	11.1	25.8
Back spaces	1.1	1.0	1.7	0.6	8.2	12.6
Yards	0.6	0.8	0.2	0.2	2.4	4.2
Park/alley	0.5	0.2	1.5	0.4	5.5	8.4

street. People were categorized by age-group, sex, location, and activity, using the same activity categories and breakdown into *recreational* and *non-recreational* activities that were used for the walking census.

The driving census was repeated 38 times, at least twice each week, from May through August. Twenty-nine counts were made on alternating weekdays (10 mornings, 9 afternoons, 10 evenings); and nine counts were made on weekends (3 mornings, 3 afternoons, and 3 evenings). In the 38 drives, over 84,000 entries were made, an average of 2210 entries per census.

The findings showed that adults were the largest single group of recreators, but they were not well represented in the parks. Teenagers were only 16 percent of the population, but they accounted for almost 30 percent of those observed in the parks. Most adult and teenage recreators were male, and 90 percent of the teenagers in the park were male. Just over half the users of the parks were children. The majority of recreators were, then, on the streetfront, where they outnumbered the pedestrians. Most recreators on the streetfront were sitting and talking, or playing. (See Table 9.4.)

Table 9.3   Walking Census: Percentage Composition of People Recreating in the Park, in Average Park Block, by Time of Day, by Age/Sex Groupings

Time	Men	Women	Teen Boys	Teen Girls	Children	Total
All-time average	6.2	2.6	18.4	4.3	68.5	100%
1.30 p.m.	6.9	3.5	16.4	4.4	69.0	100%
5.00 p.m.	5.6	1.5	20.0	4.2	68.7	100%

Table 9.4   Driving Census: Number of People Observed Out of Doors (Average number per census)

	Recreation		Non-recreation	
	Streetfront	Parks	Working	Pedestrian
Adults	589	13	20	553
Men	<u>339</u>	<u>9</u>		
Women	250	4		
Teens	169	31	3	182
Boys	<u>96</u>	<u>27</u>		
Girls	<u>73</u>	4		
Children	399	47	2	205
Total	1,157	91	25	940

BLOCK PROFILES

Nine blocks were selected for case studies. The methods in each block used included interviews, a walking census, resident diaries, and a survey of known neighbors.

Walking Census

The walking census was described earlier. In the case study blocks a different schedule of observations was used. Here the census was repeated three days a week (on alternating days each week) over a period of six to eight weeks. The walking census was repeated four times during each observation day: 10:00 a.m., 1:30 p.m., 5 p.m., and 8 p.m. Census takers included staff members, students, and local residents.

Interviews

At each study site between fourteen and twenty residents were interviewed using a standard interview form. Participants were asked questions about attitudes and circumstances that might affect their use of outdoor space.

Residents' Diaries

Participants in each of the study blocks kept diaries of their outdoor activities over a two month period. Diaries were kept for three days a week on alternating days each week, and different days were assigned to different participants in the same block. On each diary day, the participant recorded the location, nature, and duration of outdoor activities for each member of the family. Predated diary forms (separate forms for mornings, afternoons, and evenings) were handed to each participant each week.

Survey of Known Neighbors

As part of the interview, participants were shown a composite photograph of the house facades on their street and around the block, and they were asked to identify, by name or description, who lived in each house. For each person or household that participants were able to identify, they were asked several questions to establish the nature and frequency of their interactions. For example, they were asked about family relationship, friendship, borrowing and lending things, exchanging favors, taking care of children, discussing problems, and membership in civic, religious, and social organizations.

Fremont Avenue Block

The Fremont Avenue block contains 43 row houses, several stores, and a church. The houses along one side of the block are two stories high and single occupancy. The other houses in the block are three stories, and most have been subdivided into three or more apartments. All the houses have small, fenced backyards. An alley runs through the block from north to south; it connects to a narrower alley, and the two alleys define two sides of a quarter-acre inner-block park. The other two sides of the park are defined by abutting back yards. The park is paved and contains several items of play equipment.

Trash accumulation was a subject of general concern. Systematic ratings of conditions in the block over a ten-week period showed the park to be in worse condition than the other outdoor spaces. Residents put their trash in the alley alongside the park where it was scattered by dogs, children, and the wind. Twenty backyards were selected at random for observations: nineteen were used for trash storage, eighteen were used for clothes drying, five had seats, and three had play equipment.

There were 117 observations between July and September. About half of the people observed in the census were recreating; the other half were pedestrians or engaged in some kind of work. Despite the presence of an inner-block park, most recreational activity occurred on the streetfront. With an average of 22.2 people recreating in the block per census, 6.7 were in the back spaces (the park and yards) and 15.5 were on the streetfront. The intensity of recreational activity was not even throughout the day. On the streetfront the numbers increased continuously from an average of 7.1 at 10 a.m. to 26.9 at 8 p.m. In the back spaces, there were an average of 5.3 people at 10 a.m.; this figure went up to 7 at 1:30 p.m. and then it showed little change for the rest of the day. The

17   Fremont Avenue Block

This photograph shows an aerial view of the inner-block park. Photograph courtesy of Baltimore City Department of Planning.

intensity of non-recreational activity did not vary much through the day, so that the people who were recreating increased from 40 percent of the total at 10 a.m. to 61 percent at 8 p.m.

Of the people recreating on the park, 83 percent were children. In the mornings there were more children in the park than on the streetfront; by midday there were twice as many children in the park as there were on the street. In the afternoon, however, the number of children in the park decreased slightly while the number in the street increased sharply, so that by 8 p.m. there were 5.2 children in the park and 9.0 on the streetfront. Teenage boys used the playground in the late afternoons and evenings. At all periods of the day, then, there were more people recreating along the front than in the interior of the block. The difference in intensity between front and back spaces increased dramatically during the late afternoon and evening. (See Table 9.5.)

Fourteen adult residents of the Fremont Avenue block kept diaries of their outdoor activities during the same eight-week period that observations were being made. The most frequently mentioned activities were *playing* and *sitting and talking;* 62 percent of these sitting and talking incidents and 32 percent of the playing incidents took place on the streetfront.

Table 9.5   Walking Census of Fremont Avenue Block: People Recreating by Location in the Block, by Time of Day, by Age/Sex Groupings (Average number of people per census)

Time	Men	Women	Teen Boys	Teen Girls	Children	All People
Streetfront						
10.00 a.m.	2.59	1.59	0.52	0.28	2.08	7.06
1.30 p.m.	3.33	1.50	0.61	0.77	3.10	9.31
5.00 p.m.	3.21	3.72	2.17	2.66	6.97	18.72
8.00 p.m.	3.10	5.69	4.97	4.10	9.00	26.86
Inner-block spaces						
10.00 a.m.	0.10	1.10	0.34	0.17	3.90	5.30
1.30 p.m.	0.00	0.30	0.17	0.03	6.53	7.03
5.00 p.m.	0.03	0.20	0.62	0.10	6.45	7.40
8.00 p.m.	0.10	0.17	1.45	0.07	5.20	6.99

In interviews, residents indicated that they did not sit out in the back. They felt, however, that the presence of the park made the block more attractive. They characterized the park as safer and cleaner than the street for children to play. It also had the advantage of keeping the children away from the adults who were sitting on the streetfront. The major disadvantages were fighting among the children, the presence of undesirables like addicts and alcoholics, and the constant presence of trash. People who did not themselves have young children were more likely to complain about the noise and trash in the back and about rough children taking over the park.

Fourteen residents were asked to identify their neighbors and to characterize the nature of their interactions with them. Analysis shows that the average resident knew 17 neighbors and was on talking terms with all of them; 11 lived on the same street and the other six lived around the block. Seven of the known neighbors were considered friends (five of them lived on the same street), two were on borrowing/lending terms (both lived on the same street), and there was one (who lived on the same street) with whom childcare services were exchanged. Despite the presence of a park in the middle of the block, residents' social interactions were mainly with the people who lived on their street.

BRUCE MANOR APARTMENTS

Bruce Manor Apartments were constructed in 1969 on a two acre site. They consist of 110 apartments in four buildings arranged around a central parking lot. On the street side, each building is separated from the sidewalk by a twenty-foot grass strip, with paths leading through the grass to each of the building entrances.

The parking lot is paved with blacktop; it connects with the street at two points, and is designed to accommodate 102 cars. Trash storage units are located in the center of the parking lot, together with a climber and a basketball net.

Each building has four floors, with three and a half floors above ground level. Four units on each floor share a stair hall, two units facing the street and two facing the parking lot. At the bottom of each stair hall there are two entrance doors to the building, with a short flight of exterior stairs to the sidewalk on one side and the parking lot on the other. Most of the units have either two or three bedrooms, and all are air-conditioned. The rents are subsidized. Most of the residents of Bruce Manor moved in from the surrounding neighborhoods. There were a total of 408 residents, including 138 children under the age of three, and 69 teenagers.

There is a two-thirds-acre park immediately adjacent to Bruce Manor. It has a fenced play area for tots, and a central play area with climbing mounds, a wooden ziggurat, some benches and tables. A grassy bank with trees defines the park on three sides and separates it from the street; the fourth side is one of the apartment buildings. The park was built at the same time as Bruce Manor, and it was intended primarily to serve the residents of the apartments.

There were 69 observations of the apartment building and the park between July and September. They showed that far more recreation took place on the streetfront and parking lot than in the park. Only 18 percent of the children who were out recreating were in the park. Analysis of the observations by time period showed that children were the primary users of the park in the mornings, but in the afternoons and evenings the teenagers took over. (See Table 9.6.)

Ten adult residents of Bruce Manor kept diaries of their outdoor activities over an eight-week period that coincided with the observations. The major recreational activities listed were *sitting out* and *playing*; 83 percent of sitting-out incidents and 55 percent of playing incidents took place in the front and the back of the building.

In interviews, residents expressed reservations about letting their children play in the park. The parking lot was not a safe playspace because cars tended to shoot in and out, but there were more problems in the park. There was always "a lot of hassle" because older children, many of them "from other areas," took over the park. They fought with the younger children, pushed them off the equipment, and threw things. At night, teenagers used the park for courting. In addition, children in the park fought among themselves over the use of the equipment. The parking lot had the advantage of a central location: it was

18 Bruce Manor Apartments

The parking lot is in the center. A portion of the adjacent playground is visible in the front right corner of the picture. Photograph courtesy of Baltimore City Department of Planning.

Table 9.6   Walking Census of Bruce Manor Apartments: People Recreating (Average number of people per census)

	Park	Courtyard	Streetfront	All Places
Adults	0.2	1.8	2.1	4.1
Teenagers	2.0	2.7	1.3	6.0
Children	1.7	4.8	2.8	9.3
Total	3.9	9.3	6.2	19.4

surrounded by apartments on all four sides, which meant that mothers in half the units in the project could keep an eye on the children at play. The park, on the other hand, was only visible from one of the buildings, and the view was obscured by the trees.

Adults said that they spent less time out of doors because the units were air conditioned, but they said that the children were not affected in the same way. Many said that when they wanted to socialize they went out onto the steps, preferably the front steps. (There was a management restriction against sitting on the front steps—the manager said that it "made a bad impression.") When asked why they chose to sit out on the front steps, residents commented: more scenery, others are there, friends sit there, children enjoy it, and habit. People also sat on the steps that faced the parking lot, and they gave the following reasons for sitting there: the manager says you can't sit in the front, more space, you don't have to worry about breaking windows (the back windows were protected by grills), it's close to home, you can see the children from indoors when they play there. Some residents complained that when they were sitting on the steps they had constantly to get up and move for people entering and leaving the building; others complained that it was difficult getting in and out of the building because people were always blocking the steps.

RUTTER STREET BLOCK

The Rutter Street block is one of two sites studied in a middle-income neighborhood. Rutter Street is a narrow inner-block street; at one time there were some small houses along it, but these were demolished and a small park was created in their place. The park is bounded by Rutter Street on one side, and on the other three sides by alleys serving the yards of the houses that face outward toward the main streets. A brick wall separates Rutter Street from the park. The other side of the street is lined by yards and the backs of houses. The houses in the block are three stories high, and some of them have been extensively

19   Rutter Street Block

The park is not heavily used, but abutting residents enjoy looking out at it. Photograph by the author.

renovated. The park has a brick paved surface with several planting beds; there is a small shelter, some benches, and a water fountain whose operation is controlled by the surrounding residents who take turns keeping the key. There is no play equipment. In the next block there is a public elementary school with a large playfield.

There were 110 observations between August and October. They showed that almost two-thirds of the people recreating out of doors were in the park. About half of the park users were children; the remainder were about equally divided between adults and teenagers. About one third of all adults were in the yards, compared with 12 percent of children and 5 percent of teenagers. While the park was relatively well used, the actual intensity of outdoor activity was very low. (See Table 9.7.)

Thirteen adult residents of the Rutter Street block kept diaries of their outdoor activities over an eight-week period that coincided with the observations. The major activities recorded were *sitting and talking* and *playing*. Of all the incidents of sitting-out, 83 percent took place around the house (54 percent in the back of the house), and 58 percent of play incidents took place around the

Table 9.7   Walking Census of Rutter Street Block: People Recreating (Average number of people per census)

	Park	Backyards	Streetfront	All Places
Adults	0.3	0.3	0.3	0.9
Teenagers	0.3	0.0	0.1	0.4
Children	1.0	0.1	0.0	1.1
Total	1.6	0.4	0.4	2.4

house (44 percent in the back). People in the middle-income area were more likely than people in Harlem Park to use the back spaces for recreation.

In interviews, it was apparent that people who lived around the Rutter Street playground liked it: many felt responsible for its condition and use. Residents commented that because the park had no equipment, and because it had a boundary wall, it was easy to supervise young children playing there. Residents considered their block to be more sociable and friendly than others in the neighborhood, and much of this was attributed to the park, which provided a reason and an opportunity for getting together on a regular basis. Their feelings for the playground were in marked contrast to those for the school playground, which they felt was unsafe. They talked of incidents of rough play, theft, and intimidation.

Residents expressed a general fear of being alone outdoors. If they went out at all they preferred to remain in the block, or they took their dogs, and they avoided alleys and dark places. Because of this feeling, they were very apprehensive about anyone who appeared to be "lurking" in the park, and were on the lookout for "undesirable elements" or "gangs of kids" who could take over the park. Fortunately, there had been no incidents.

The thing that bothered residents most was noise, particularly noise made by children and automobiles. They were also bothered by dogs, bicycle riding in the park, and kids playing music late at night.

Residents enjoyed sitting in their backyards because of the privacy. In addition, they could supervise children playing in the park. The back rooms in many of the houses around the park had been opened up so that residents could enjoy a view of the park, and as a consequence the recreational use of these rooms had increased.

RESIDENTS SPEAK OUT

The following excerpts are taken from letters and from interviews with children who live in Harlem Park. Some of the interviews took the form of doll-play, where elementary school-age children were asked to reenact the kinds of play activities that they engaged in around the neighborhood using dolls and a three-dimensional set. The set consisted of a felt base, about four feet square, with colored strips to represent streets, alleys, and yards. The "houses" were open-top boxes with rowhouse facades. There were cut-out cars, and a loose square of green felt that could be placed to represent a playground. The dolls were small, flexible rubber dolls, available commercially in families of four: mother, father, boy, and girl.

Initially, the doll-play involved two researchers (an interviewer and a recorder) who went out to a participant's home and worked with a single child. Seventeen children between the ages of eight and twelve were interviewed in this way. Three years later, the doll-play was repeated at an elementary school with children from first through sixth grade, working with two children at a time and, in this way, relying more on interplay between children than between child and interviewer. Interviews were conducted with twenty-five pairs of children. The interviews were recorded on videotape. (See Photograph 20.)

The children were sent over in pairs by their class teacher. The model was set up on the floor. The children were told that their help was needed to put together a film about children's play; that the dolls would be used to represent children like themselves, and the set to represent a neighborhood similar to their own. The set was modified (for example, the playground was relocated, a vacant lot created, a store introduced) where children indicated that this would make it more like their neighborhood. Each boy was given a boy-doll and each girl a girl-doll, and the doll was given a name. The two dolls were represented as friends who lived across the street from one another. Houses were selected, and parents and a couple of friends were placed in their respective houses.

The interviewer asked the children what kinds of things they would have the dolls do, and this led to a discussion of the kinds of things the children themselves did, and what various spaces were "good" for. The children practiced speaking for the various actors (including the parents) to see what they would "sound" like. When the children indicated that they were ready to begin the game, the interviewer withdrew and the cameraman was called over. Each video session lasted between fifteen and twenty minutes. Afterwards, the children watched the videotape.

Transcripts from the Doll-Play Study

(Children spoke for the dolls, and so the names used in this transcript are the names they have given the doll-characters. Sometimes, however, the interviewer spoke directly to the children, and underlined names will be used to indicate that the children were speaking for themselves.)

Girls, First Grade:

(ZELDA and TRACY are playing in the playground.)

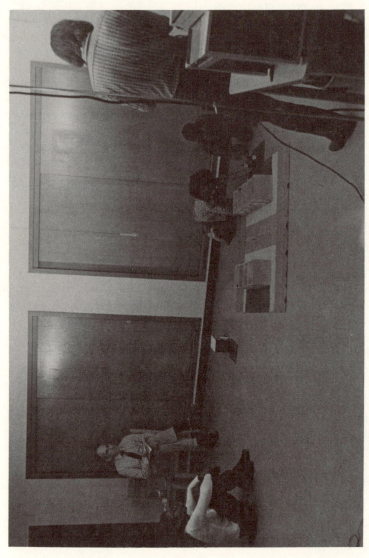

20 Doing the Doll-Play

Two boys are at the model set. Others present are the cameraman (back to camera) and two members of the study staff. Photograph courtesy of Baltimore City Department of Planning.

Interviewer: Let's say now, while you're on the swings, a bunch of new kids come in—other kids come in besides Zelda and Tracy. . . . What do you think they'll play then?

Zelda: Tracy, let's go home. There's too much children around.

Tracy: OK, let's go.

Interviewer: Is that normally what you do when a lot of kids come to the playground. Do you usually go home then?

Zelda: Yes.

Interviewer: You don't stay when they come? Why not?

Zelda: They fight too much.

Boys, Second Grade:

Mother: Milton, don't run in the street. When you see a car coming, let it go by, hear?

Milton: Yes.

Mother: Same thing goes for you, young James.

James: Yes ma'am.

Boy, Third Grade:

Zachary (TALKING ABOUT THE PARK): I can't go out there no more.

Interviewer: Why can't you go out there no more?

Zachary: They keep beating me up.

Interviewer: Wow! Who keeps beating you up?

Zachary: Wayne, Stanley, Dwight . . . he cusses.

Interviewer: Are they boys that are older than you or your age?

Zachary: Older.

Interviewer: About how old are they?

Zachary: I don't know.

Interviewer: Did you decide that you wouldn't go out there and play any more or did your mother tell you?

Zachary: My mother.

Boy, Fourth Grade:

Interviewer: What happens when you are playing in the playground and some big kids come along?

Franklin: They start a fight and chase us off the swings and slides. I go to my mom and tell her they're going to mess with me.

Interviewer: Where do they come from?

Franklin: Across the street and around the corner.

Girl, Fourth Grade:

Antonese: Here come the big children. Those wise guys! Let's hurry, they will start a fight.

21   Scene from the Doll-Play Tape

"Miss Dorothy, your son keeps picking with my boy. Can you do something to your boy? Your son needs a good whipping, that's what he needs." Photograph courtesy of Baltimore City Department of Planning.

22   Scene from the Doll-Play Tape

"Hi, Susan, Hi Maryjane. You all want to play something?"
"Yea, like what?" Photograph courtesy of Baltimore City Department of Planning.

(THEY GO HOME. MOTHER COMES OVER TO THE PLAYGROUND)

Mother: You are always here starting a fight! Why don't you leave our children alone? You'll get smacked, hear! Just watch that mouth!

Girls, Fourth Grade:

(LISA FALLS OFF THE MONKEY POLES WHILE PLAYING IN THE PARK)

Janetta: Are you hurt bad?

Lisa: No, I just skinned my knee. I'm going in the house, my knee hurts. (GOES HOME) Mother, I just fell off and hurt my knee!

Mother: How many times did I tell you about those monkey poles? Let me put a bandage on your knee.

Boy, Fourth Grade:

Father: Watch out for the car! Are you all right?

William: Yes, I guess so.

Father: I'm telling you to keep safe and watch out for all these cars. From now on you stay on the sidewalk and don't walk out into the street! . . . If you want to cross the street, go to the corner, not in the middle! Where did Bob cross over? He crossed in the middle of the street, didn't he?

William: Yes.

Father: From now on you cross in the corner, like this. If you see a car coming, you wait till the light is changed and then you walk! The light turns red—go ahead over there; but if it turns green, stop! The car might hit you. Wait till the light is red.

Boys, Fifth Grade:

Interviewer (INTRODUCING THE DOLLS): Since we have a mother and a father we should figure out some things that the mother and father might say to Freddy and Johnny when they're playing. Maybe, if they're playing in the playground and the mother and father come out, what kinds of things would they say?

Freddy: Don't cut your hand.

Johnny: Don't go too far away from home.

Boys, Fifth Grade:

John: Let's go in that neighborhood!

Fred: I'm scared of this alley. The dog might get us.

John: Yes, it's too dark anyway.

Fred: Let's run through real fast! (THEY RUN) Arf! Arf!

John: I see a dog! Come on!

Fred: Arf! Arf! Here he comes! He's coming real fast! Let's go in this old house!

John: I'm scared he might come in here and get us.

Fred: I hear a ghost! I'm getting out of here! (THEY RUN HOME) Whew, made it!

John: Yup!

Boys, Sixth Grade:

Wayne (TO WESLEY): Want to beat up on Tom and Joe?

(WAYNE AND WESLEY FIGHT TOM AND JOE)

Tom: I'll tell your mother! (GOES HOME) I'll tell my mother.

Mother: What happened to you, Tom?

Tom: Wes and Wayne started pickin' on me.

Mother: Why didn't you tell his mother?

Tom: His mother ain't home.

Boys, Sixth Grade:

(IN THE RECREATION CENTER)

Little Baby: There's those two little punks. Let's get them! They snitched on us!

Big Baby: No fighting here! We'll take care of this business outside in the back.

Bob: What shall we do now?

Davy: Let's sneak out the front door, they won't know it.

Interviewer: Do you find that you run into that much trouble with kids every day?

Bob: Uh-huh!

Interviewer: Where does most of it usually happen?

Bob: Over there by seventy-eight, where all them big kids at. They start fights. They bike people.

Interviewer: About how old are these kids?

Bob: Fifteen, fourteen.

Letter from Queen, an 11 Year Old Girl

(As part of an attempt to bring residents of the Harlem Avenue block closer together, the study staff organized a block newsletter. This letter was submitted for publication.)

To whom this may concern:

My name is Queen Young, and I'm eleven years old. While I was visiting my grandmother this summer the two playgrounds in the back of the 1100 block of Harlem Avenue were not fit for children to play in because the grownups drink in them and the teenagers won't let the small children alone. I think that someone older should be there with the small ones every day, and I think that these places should be cleaned once a week. Because when I was on the sliding board one of the steps came off when I was on it and I almost broke my neck. When I got on the monkey pole it began to shake and I almost fell down again, and the things on the playground should be fix so children will not hurt themselves.

Queen Young

Excerpts from an Interview with Michael, an 11 Year Old Boy

Michael: [We played in the yard] while Mr. Robinson was gone 'cause his wife died. We took and tore down the tree.

Interviewer: That was in the yard?

Michael: Uh-huh.

Interviewer: Was he pleased with that?

Michael: It weren't his tree, it was the landlord's tree. You see, the landlord he always blames things on . . . me and my friends. That's why we took the tree down.

Michael: [My mother] let me play on the front in summer cause in the back [in the park] it be the older boys and girls . . . kissin' and stuff, and she don't like us to be around.

Interviewer: So in the summer in the evenings you play on the sidewalk?

Michael: Yes sir.

Interviewer: Where is the best place to go to for excitement?

Michael: In the playground.

Interviewer: What kind of excitement do you see there?

Michael: At night-time you see excitement—dope addicts and stuff, and we find dope . . . and you see fights all the time on the playground.

Interviewer: Do you go out there at night?

Michael: Sometimes I do at night, but sometimes I don't; but if I don't go out on the playground at night, I look out my window and see what's going on; and then, if nobody else sees it, next morning I report it. That's what we do if nobody else see it: we tell each other.

Interviewer: You mean you tell your friends?

Michael: Yes sir.

Michael: [The best place to go skating is] down Harlem Avenue 'cause we got a nice hill— it's smooth. Or we can go down Shields Place—it's a little street with no cars running down. When you skate down, you go to Hoffman Street, turn right on Hoffman Street, go up Argyle Avenue, come back up Dolphin, and go down it again. . . . I stop before I get to [Myrtle Avenue]. I hold my feet like *that* [GESTURES] and it slows me up and I can see what cars are coming, and if no cars [are] coming we just go straight across.

Letters to *The Sun* Newspaper

(These two letters to the Editor were probably not written by residents of Harlem Park, but they might have been, and they show two sides of a problem that is common in inner-city neighborhoods.)

June 16, 1971

SIR: I am 13 years old. I have a younger brother and two younger sisters. We have a problem. We don't have a place to play.

All the neighbors complain. We can't play out front or out back. We can't even play in the parks nearby. We can't play ball or ride bikes in the parks because boys play on baseball teams. The leaders say we disturb the boys.

We can't play ball out front because it hits the other people's car. Most people have new cars too.

We can't play ball out back because it goes in the other people's yards and they won't let us get it. We can't ride bikes anywhere because the neighbors are afraid we will hit their car.

We can't stay in the house all the time. What can we do?

JODIE ANN COONEY, Baltimore

August 3, 1971

SIR: Isn't it time for mothers (and fathers too) to take a firm stand on the conduct of their children? I see parents sitting on their steps watching their children run wild all over people's cars, playing ball on their lawns, pulling up flowers and destroying their window boxes, climbing and tearing down the beautiful trees. What is it with these people?

Parents, who are legally responsible for their children, should be made to answer to a court of justice for allowing the rights of others to be forever invaded. In-town living is now at an all-time low. There is nothing but hostility and resentment all around. Maybe if the police could get back on a "beat" there might be some sign of order—or have the people who know it all hollered "police brutality" so loud that the kids think they are brutal?

Now that school is out and parents are in they are deaf, blind and very dumb to the children's behavior. Let's be neighborly and stop allowing these future monsters to destroy us.

MERLE O. LANE, Baltimore

INTERVENTIONS

The Harlem Park studies were intended not only to collect data but also to improve existing conditions, and so there were a number of attempts to intervene in the affairs of the neighborhood. This is an account of three of these interventions: what we tried to do and what actually happened. It illustrates some of the issues associated with the process of design in Harlem Park. In this account the names of the participants have been changed to protect their privacy.

Harlem Avenue Block: Excerpts from Staff Notes

The Harlem Avenue site is a triangular block consisting of 54 three-story and 24 two-story row houses. There are 98 housing units, 28 of which are owner-occupied. Two alleys run behind the backyards and connect with the surround-

23   Harlem Avenue Block

The aerial view shows the grassy park in the center. Photograph courtesy of Baltimore City Department of Planning.

ing streets at three points. In the center of the block there is a triangular piece of land, about one-tenth of an acre in size. An old laundry building had stood on this land, but it was demolished and at the time the study began the triangular inner-block parcel was vacant and unimproved. The residents of the block wanted the City to build a park on the vacant land. A park would be an improvement over what had stood there before. It would provide a place for children to play away from the traffic and removed from the adults on the streetfront. The City agreed to build the park.

In preparation, the City made a study of the outdoor spaces in the block. The study found that most recreation took place on the streetfront and not in the back (an average of 22 people recreated on the sidewalks, and 7 in the back). Ball playing was the most popular activity on the vacant lot. Sixteen residents were interviewed: thirteen said that they were fearful of going out alone at night; they cited danger, crime, drug addicts, bad people, robbers, and alcoholics. Nine respondents had young children, and eight of them said that they did not allow their children to play outside the block. Noise was given as the major source of disturbance, and children and teenagers were given as the major source of noise. Most respondents indicated that even with a park in the back they expected that they themselves would continue to sit out on the streetfront. While they were generally in favor of a park, they did anticipate some disadvantages: fighting among children, the presence of outsiders in the block, more noise, and the tendency for rough children to take over.

Members of the Planning Department staff met with a committee of residents. They presented the findings of their study and discussed its implications for the design of the park. Initially the group had wanted a "passive park"; now they decided to proceed in two phases. The first phase would be an experimental year: the site would be cleared and grassed, and agency staff would assist residents to develop satisfactory uses in the space. This effort would serve as the basis for phase two, when final development plans would be prepared and implemented.

The the land was cleared, levelled and grassed, and immediately kids began to play ball there. What follows are edited excerpts from staff notes about activities during the experimental year.

In the Harlem Avenue block we were determined that something should happen, so we printed over 250 flyers advertising "a big block meeting" to discuss the use and care of the park. Our intention was to elicit from residents the kinds of things they would like to see happen in the park, and to see if they would be willing to lead in these activities.

About 150 residents showed up in the park for the meeting. Baked goods, drinks, and cookies, made by block residents, were laid out on a table.

There was some difficulty getting everyone together so that the meeting could get started. A staff member explained the general purpose of the meeting, and then a sort of "free for all" verbal exchange developed. Mrs. Elma Baker said that the park should only cater to children under the age of ten or twelve years; it could only meet the play needs of the tots. Some equipment, such as swings and bars, should be put in by the City. From there on the meeting literally came apart. Two main interest groups seemed to emerge: the older homeowners on the one hand, and the young adults and teenagers on the other. Older residents and homeowners complained that teenagers who played basketball and baseball were a menace in the park. One homeowner was particularly upset that stray balls kept coming over the fence into her backyard. When this happened, a teenager would either climb over her fence to retrieve the ball (which angered her the most), or she would have to constantly go and get the ball for them. Other complaints from homeowners included excessive noise and loitering.

The teenagers' main concern was that they needed somewhere to play, and the most convenient place was in their own block. They also said that they would rather play in the park than in the street. When asked what facilities they thought were needed, they said that this open space had served quite well up to that point.

Young adults, especially those with small children, sided with the teenagers. They felt that the park should serve as an area for all age groups to play. However, they said, they would like to see some portable equipment, which would serve the tots better than simply an open space.

After about forty-five minutes of shouting, the residents drifted into small groups, each group discussing the issue that was of most importance to it. While these factions were engaged in discussion, refreshments were served. The meeting ended informally as individuals gradually departed.

On the plus side, we were able at least to get names of teenagers, children, and adults who voiced an interest in exploring the possibility of working together to improve the park. Members of the project staff arranged to meet with the teenagers.

On the whole, the meeting seemed to have done more harm than good. The state of "undeclared war" between homeowners and the newer influx of younger residents was now out in the open, and for a time it seemed we had really opened a Pandora's box that we were not able to control.

The teenagers selected a member of their group, Ms. Shelly Highland, to meet with the project staff. She had been articulate at the meeting, had lived in the community all her life, and knew virtually all of the teenagers in the block. We raised the possibility of teenagers doing things in the park.

We suggested some way of making money—say, a carwash—so as to buy equipment, such as balls and a net. Shelly was pessimistic about getting the adult residents to allow them to take water because that would add to their water bill. Furthermore, they expected the City to provide play equipment; they should not have to pay for it. She said the teenagers wanted the right to use the park two evenings a week. They would play volley-ball, basketball, badminton, and baseball. They would also make plans for a cook-out. Their immediate need was for some benches and a basketball hoop.

Meanwhile two prominent younger residents of the block suggested showing movies in the park. The staff secured the use of the Planning Department's projector, and a member of the staff accompanied Ms. Highland and another resident, Mr. Barton, to the Enoch Pratt library to select and reserve films. Flyers were circulated on the block advertising that movies would be shown in the park on Thursday evenings. The first Thursday there were some seventy-five people, about half of them children and the rest about evenly split between teenagers and adults. A number of people brought chairs; others sat on the grass or leaned against the fences. There was excitement in the air. Most of the audience stayed through the entire hour and a half, and they applauded at the end.

The second Thursday there was a similarly enthusiastic crowd, smaller in number but with more adults. At the beginning the block leader made a short speech, commending Ms. Highland and Mr. Barton for their efforts. She presented them with a personal donation of five dollars toward the cost of future programs. Refreshments were provided for the kids. Three films were shown. The last film was rather dull. Several small boys began throwing stones causing some of the adults to leave.

By the time the third week came around, problems had developed as a result of other activities in the park. The audience was small. A makeshift game of basketball created a disturbance. A group of teenagers started shooting craps and one resident called the police. After the first hour, only six or seven people remained watching the movie.

There was no initiative on the part of the residents to continue with the film showings, and so the program was terminated.

During this same time, Ms. Highland and Mr. Barton had organized the youngsters in the block into baseball teams. In the past, although baseball games had been a regular feature of the park, they had been loosely organized and would occur at inappropriate times. Now, under the leadership of these two residents, the games were more structured. There were regular playing times—in the evenings—and there was talk of purchasing uniforms and new equipment. In conjunction with this activity, a regular clean-up was being undertaken two mornings a week. The Bureau of Recreation supplied brooms and trash cans. This brought a totally new atmosphere to the park. The park was in excellent shape.

24   Ball-Playing on the Harlem Avenue Block

Photograph courtesy of Baltimore City Department of Planning.

The ball-playing was suspended because of an incident that occurred one Saturday afternoon. The story was that a ball had gone over a fence several times that afternoon, and the owner of the house decided to impound the ball. One of the players then threatened to break a window if the ball was not released. The owner called the block leader. We do not know just how the incident was eventually resolved, but on Monday morning, the block leader called the Director of the Department of Recreation and Parks, the police, and the Department of Planning. She also called Mrs. Ena Brown, the president of the neighborhood association, who then met with Ms. Highland, Mr. Barton, and the project staff.

For the most part Mrs. Brown was favorable to the activities in the park, but she had to pacify both sides. She called an emergency meeting of the neighborhood planning committee to discuss the issue. Fifteen block residents, including Ms. Highland and Mr. Barton, were present at the meeting. One man complained bitterly that he was on night shift and that the ball playing and the noise disturbed his sleep. He said that his home was his castle, and he should not be disturbed in this way. Most of the other homeowners said that the space was just too small for ball playing. Two adults joined with two or three youngsters who had shown up for the meeting to support the play activity. They felt that children should be able to engage in some kind of constructive activity near home. Mrs. Walker said that if the play activity were stopped, within a few days the open space would be in "terrible condition," as it had been before the start of the summer.

The meeting ended in a compromise: the youngsters could carry out the remainder of the activities they had planned for the summer (the movies, a cookout, and a fashion show), but there should be no ball playing of any kind.

By this time Ms. Highland and Mr. Barton had lost interest in continuing their leadership role. The complained that they were not getting paid for their efforts. They were volunteering their time and energy and some of their money, and having to take this much flak from older residents—who, they said, were not doing anything for the block—was more than they could stand.

When the ball playing stopped, the incentive for the clean-up program stopped too. The park showed signs of deterioration and the usual accumulation of trash and broken glass began to collect.

The following year, residents showed no interest in continuing to work on the design of the park, and so it remained as it was—a level, grassy lot.

"Liven the Parks"

There were many social clubs in Harlem Park. One of these clubs was known as Fellow Jets; its members were a group of young men who had grown up around block 97 in Harlem Park. Some of them had moved away, but they felt an attachment for the old neighborhood and came back to visit almost every day. They were an energetic group. At a block meeting called by the study staff to discuss the condition of the parks, a leader of the Fellow Jets complained that the park was in bad condition and he offered to paint it if the City would supply the necessary equipment and supplies. The project staff asked the Department of Recreation and Parks for paints, brushes, rollers, and masking tape, and the young men began a massive paint-up.

To fully appreciate the impact of their work one would have had to visit the park during the month of August. The jungle gyms were painted white with red polka-dots, and there were drawings and slogans painted all over the paving. Cartoons were carefully reproduced from comic books, and characters like Fred Flintstone, Olive Oyl, and Tweetie Bird had "balloons" coming out of their mouths urging users to keep the park clean. On any day while this activity was in progress, a host of adults and young children could be seen sweeping and cleaning in the park. City officials were shown around and they were complimentary. Within a month or so, word had spread to the next-door block and a number of young residents there met to organize a similar clean-up in their park. There was clearly a feeling of competition.

Resident participation in block 97 was enthusiastic, but it lasted only as long as there was outside support. There was a high level of activity throughout the summer, but during the fall it decreased and during the winter litter and trash began to cover over the designs on the paving. Nevertheless, the project staff felt that the intervention had been successful and they decided to apply what they had learned. The key elements in getting residents involved in park main-

25   Resident-Generated Improvements in the Park

Residents painted cartoon figures on the pavement as part of an effort to improve the park in their block. Photograph courtesy of Baltimore City Department of Planning.

26   Children Got Involved in Park Improvements

Photograph courtesy of Baltimore City Department of Planning.

tenance seemed to be competition; encouragement, assistance, and recognition from outside; and an activity that could be characterized as fun rather than duty.

During the winter months the staff worked with the Department of Recreation and Parks and residents of Harlem Park to organize a competition for the best-maintained inner-block park. The following summer a competition called "Liven the Parks" was opened to all residents of Harlem Park. A panel of judges was appointed. The City provided brooms, spades, paint, seeds, and trashbags for participating groups; and prizes for the three blocks that showed the greatest improvement over the period of the competition: a party with food, games, and music in the park. In addition, there were prizes cups and certificates for individual effort.

The "Liven the Parks" competition was well received, and it brought about increased use and active participation by residents in many of the inner-block parks, but the following summer the City did not revive the competition and the parks returned to their former state.

AN EXPERIMENT WITH RESIDENT MANAGEMENT

Between 1980 and 1983 a concerted attempt was made to introduce resident-management in the inner-block parks. This was a response to the earlier studies, which had showed that there were problems in the parks: they were a popular hangout for teenagers, alcoholics, drug users, and other groups generally regarded as threatening and undesirable; they were noisy, and they collected litter, household garbage, abandoned furniture and appliances, and broken glass. No one was in charge there. The parks were a no-man's land. These problems could be corrected by installing a fulltime manager or supervisor in each park, but the City could not afford to do that. The alternative was for residents who lived around the park to assume a management role.

The City submitted a proposal to the U.S. Department of the Interior for a grant to make physical improvements in eight inner-block parks in Harlem Park and to explore and implement approaches to resident management. The proposal included testing some ideas about redesigning the parks so that they would invite and facilitate resident management. (These had come out of the earlier studies; see Brower et al., 1976.) The proposal also included the transfer of certain responsibilities and rights of control in the parks from the City to an organization of local residents. This organization would participate in the redesign of the parks. Finally, the project included a research element: the validity of hypotheses about design and organization of resident-managed parks would be tested and a general model developed. Harlem Park with its twenty-nine similar parks, provided an unusual opportunity for a controlled experiment.

The project was approved in November 1980, and funded for two years. Plans for the parks would be developed during the first year, which would leave the second year for implementation and evaluation. The Department of Planning, which coordinated and administered the project for the City, contracted with

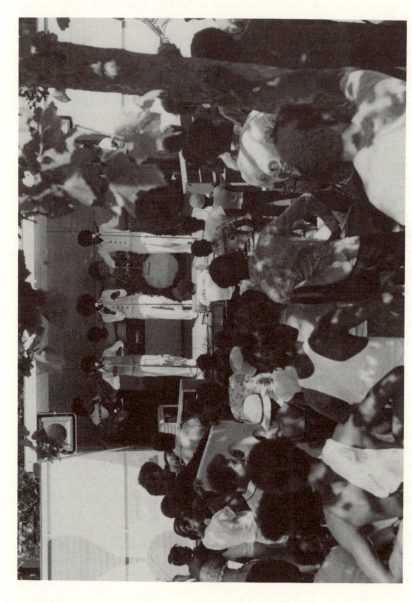

27   Liven the Parks Competition

The first prize was a party in the winning park, complete with band and cookout. Photograph courtesy of Baltimore City Department of Planning.

two local universities, one for community organization and park planning, and the other for evaluation.

The idea of community management had originated with members of the staff of the Department of Planning, and community leaders in Harlem Park had approved the idea and supported the grant application. The majority of Harlem Park residents, however, knew nothing about any of this and so when the project was funded the first task was to inform the residents. A community-wide meeting was called, but only a handful of people showed up and so it was decided to make formal presentations to the two existing community organizations in the area. The leaders of these organizations had supported the grant application, and the purposes of the presentations were to solicit nominations for eight parks to be included in the study, and to obtain a commitment to participate in the formation of a community-wide organization that would oversee the redesign of these parks. But the project staff found themselves caught up in arguments about project management—who was being employed and how much each person was being paid. After several meetings—and feeling that time was passing, the main issues were being sidetracked, and there was a schedule to meet—the staff decided to broaden their tactics: while continuing to meet with the two community organizations, they would approach other associations in the area—church groups, block clubs, youth associations, and tenant councils—and try to persuade each group to nominate one park. If eight groups could be matched up with eight parks, then these groups could form the nucleus of a community organization.

During the first two months of the project, the staff attended a great many meetings, each on the subject of a particular park. Ideas about park design and management were discussed, and suggestions were made for residents to become involved. Groups were told that if they had ideas about how the parks should be used, and if they were organized so that they could see to it that these uses would in fact take place, they would better the chances that their park would be selected for improvement. The staff made it clear that only eight parks would be selected, and that the selection would be made by a community organization that was yet to be formed. The staff offered to assist each group to get organized and to prepare a proposal.

In the fourth month, community leaders insisted on the immediate formation of a community-wide organization to oversee the project, and so a community meeting was called. This time it was well attended, and a community organization, named the Harlem Park Trust, was formed. The Trust had representatives from the two existing community organizations, the churches and schools in the area, and state and local government.

The tasks of the Trust, as the staff saw them, were to approve eight parks to participate in the project, and to encourage, oversee and participate in the design and management activities of each sponsoring group. But the Trust had other priorities. At the early meetings, issues of project management once again dominated the discussions. Members of the Trust were particularly upset that important decisions about project personnel had been made without them, and they wanted a regular accounting of all project expenditures. Discussions at the Trust meetings were heated. There was little substantive discussion about the purposes of the project, and no progress leading to their implementation. In the meantime, with the approval of the Trust, the staff continued to meet with groups in the community, soliciting nominations and helping interested groups to develop and refine their proposals.

In the eighth month of the project the Trust approved preliminary designs for eight park sites. For reasons of economy all of the parks were to go to bid as a single contract, which meant that the final designs had to be approved for all of the parks before work could begin on any one of them. The park sponsors included a church group, a tenants council, four block clubs, and the Trust itself.

There were several management models that the project staff wanted to test, but as the Trust established its place in the community it assumed responsibility for the decisions in all eight parks; and in the end, the differences in the management of the eight parks reflected group dynamics and block politics, and they did not represent controlled, predetermined variables.

The staff put their ideas about park design in the form of written guidelines and presented them to the Trust. These guidelines grew out of the findings of the earlier studies, and the staff expected that the Trust would accept and apply them. They were mistaken. The Trust saw the staff as consultants to the City, not the community. If residents were to have a say in the design of the parks, then *they* would decide what they wanted: they did not want the City to tell them what they should want. Consequently, very few of the guidelines were considered seriously.

In the thirteenth month of the project the Trust reviewed the status of the designs for all eight parks. Some significant changes were proposed in the existing parks: a new tennis court, an additional basketball court, a stage for outdoor performances, an area designed especially for the elderly, and the contruction of barriers across the alleys to block automobile access. For the first time each park was to be given a name. But in the main, the changes reflected the conventional ideas that had governed the original design of the parks, and there were no concessions to the special needs of resident management. Then members of the Trust went on a trip to New York City to look at community-managed parks there, and they had second thoughts about the designs.

By this time, according to the original schedule, the parks should have been ready to go out for bids. In order to avoid subverting the participation process, the project deadline was extended by twelve months; this would postpone the construction schedule from early spring into the summer, and shift the evaluation to the summer of the following year. But even with this extension there would be no time to spare if the parks were to go through the City's lengthy bidding process, and so it was decided to "contract-in" most of the work: the construction drawings would be handled by architects in the Department of

Planning, and construction work would be handled by the Mayor's Office of Manpower Resources under a program that provided job training for the unemployed. This meant that the work would be done by unskilled laborers, but they would be working under experienced supervisors, and they could begin immediately, before all decisions had been finalized. Instruction would be given on site as the work progressed. The Trust approved these arrangements. There would be regular monthly progress meetings attended by the city agencies involved, and by representatives of the Trust and the project staff. The Trust organized a festival, and each participating block had a booth with food, drink, arts and crafts or games. There were marching bands, and the large crowd included local politicians and city agency representatives.

Work on the parks began in mid-summer with a completion date set for the end of the year. That date was moved to spring of the following year, then to summer, then to fall, and the parks were not substantially completed until the winter, eighteen months after construction had begun. There were a number of reasons for the delay: workers were pulled off the project in order to attend to other jobs that the Administration wanted done; there were differences in interpreting the schematic drawings, and poor workmanship and choice of finishings required work to be redone and items to be taken out and replaced. In addition, the Trust came up with many new requests and revisions. Throughout the construction period the Trust participated in monthly progress meetings, but as time went on and the work remained incomplete the Trust voiced increasing dissatisfaction and frustration.

Delay in the timing of the construction work threw out the evaluation schedule. During the first summer, systematic observations in eight project and four control blocks provided a profile of the park users, and the observations were to have been repeated the following summer when the physical changes were complete. This would have enabled the evaluators to compare each block to itself and to a control block at two different points in time. But during the second summer the parks were still under construction, and so it was not possible to obtain valid "after" measures.

A household questionnaire was conducted that second summer. The original intention had been to compare the attitudes of residents on renovated blocks with those of residents on control blocks, but as the parks were still under construction at the time the interviews were done, it was decided instead to compare residents' attitudes about the past and future of the parks.

The findings showed that residents in the project blocks had a far more positive view of the future of the parks than residents in the non-project blocks. While attitudes about past problems in the parks were similar, residents in the project blocks expected fewer problems in the future, and were more inclined to rely on local resources to get help in dealing with local problems (Taylor, 1983). The survey also produced one disconcerting piece of information: after more than two years of operation, three quarters of the respondents in the project blocks had never heard of the Harlem Park Trust, and few people credited it

28   Harlem Park Trust Sign in the Park

Signs in one of the project parks announce that the improvements were sponsored by the community. It is ironic that three-quarters of the residents surveyed were unaware of the role played by the Harlem Park Trust. Photograph by the author.

with a major role in the improvement of the parks; in fact, more credit was given to local leaders and the older community organizations than to the Trust. This may have been because the local leaders had multiple memberships, so they were generally identified with their old organizations instead of with the new. The fact remains, however, that after all its efforts, the Trust was not generally known and recognized.

Toward the end of the project period the staff drafted a set of management agreements for the eight project parks. This document spelled out, for each park, which management responsibilities would remain with the City and which would be handed over to the Trust. It detailed, for example, who would do general structural repairs, clean the parks, collect the debris, post notices on the bulletin boards, replace tennis balls, store loose equipment, supervise the correct placement of household garbage, trim the trees, maintain the flowerbeds, lock the gates, replace light bulbs, and plan and operate events in the parks. The draft was intended as the first step in a negotiation process through which the City and the Trust would work out an acceptable balance of responsibility and authority. The Trust, however, refused to discuss the management agreement because it felt that the construction work had not been satisfactorily completed.

Two years later, the only project parks that were in good condition were those where block residents had taken it upon themselves to provide continuing management and supervision. The other parks were every bit as bad as they had been before.

Thinking back about the project, I believe that our main problems in Harlem Park did not occur because we had the wrong answers, but because at the time we had the answers to the wrong questions. We stressed the importance of product, when we should have stressed the process of social learning. We tried to tell the community what to do to avoid the mistakes of the past, but these were not their mistakes, and it was not their past. They had to experience the mistakes for themselves before they were ready to invest in experimental solutions. We presented ideas for designing parks that were easier to manage than the conventional models, but residents had yet to learn whether they could manage parks at all. Before the Trust was ready to take on the parks, it had to test the strength of the residents' commitment to the project, the limits of their own authority and power, and the balance between collective and personal interests.

10

As Residents See It

A description of the residential environment from the viewpoint of residents of Harlem Park.

STREETFRONTS

Recreation is a major use of the streetfront and the most common recreational activity on the streetfront is sitting-and-talking. Most sitting takes place on the steps and on chairs set out in front of the house, often chained to a basement window. During the day most recreators are on the shady side of the street. Their numbers increase toward the late afternoon and evening. On summer evenings the streetfronts are alive with people of all ages.

This will not come as a surprise to anyone who is familiar with the area, and it is usually assumed to be a less-than-desirable situation. A common explanation is that the houses are so hot and crowded that residents are, in essence, driven out of doors. But people sit out on the steps even when the units are air conditioned and not crowded. Another common explanation for sitting out on the front is that there is nowhere else to go: if there were adequate parks, people would not sit in the front. But people who have backyards hardly ever sit in them, and people who have easy access to public parks hardly ever sit there. In Harlem Park, where there is a park in virtually every block, the parks are used well below capacity and there are three times as many people recreating on the streetfront as in the parks. There are twice as many children on the streetfront. Adults, especially women, hardly ever use the parks.

Residents have generally positive feelings about sitting on the streetfront:

29   A Typical Streetfront Scene

Residents sit out front whether or not there is a park nearby. Photograph by the author.

they enjoy sitting out there, it is a habit, a custom, where one meets one's friends, where the action is. Security considerations have a strong influence on residents' choice of where to be, and residents feel safer on the streetfront because it is open and visible, lighted at night, and patrolled by police. The fact that other people they know recreate there adds to the sense of security and discourages potential burglars.

There are negative features about recreational use of the streetfront. Automobile traffic makes it a dangerous place for children to play. Active use of the streetfront means that there is always litter around. Constant exposure to one's neighbors means a loss of privacy—they know all one's comings and goings. Another objection to sitting on the streetfront is that it is the sign of a lower-class neighborhood: although residents choose to sit there, they feel it is not seemly—after all, one does not see people doing it in the "better" neighborhoods.

Streetfront recreation is tied to a pattern of socializing characterized by chance meetings with neighbors and passers-by, and the front, the focus for all arrivals and departures and the scene of frequent and varied activities—the arrival of street hawkers, mailmen, social workers, visitors, and the like—is the best place for this kind of socializing. This casual approach is in marked contrast with that in a middle-income area. Here residents are more likely to meet by appointment and to entertain their neighbors in the privacy of the backyard. Adults never "hang out" on the streetfront. (Their children, however, often do.)

BACK SPACES

There is a distinct difference in the way residents perceive front and back spaces. The front of the house is the public face: it is the side one presents to visitors and it reflects on one's character and respectability. The space in front of the house is the first outdoor space that residents clean, tidy, and decorate. The front also reflects on the character of the community. Residents are far more concerned about the appearance of the front of their neighbors' houses than the backs, and if there is any pressure to conform, it is directed to the front of the house.

The back spaces, in contrast, are perceived as an extension of the service side of the house. This is where one keeps the dog, hangs the washing to dry, has a vegetable or flower garden. A fence is essential for protection, but if it obstructs the view from the alley it only creates places for potential intruders to hide. A paved surface is desirable because it is easy to keep clean and because it eliminates breeding places for rats. Sometimes the paved surface is painted green, sometimes with geometric designs. There is outdoor furniture in some of the yards, but their function is more symbolic than practical: few residents actually sit there.

Because back spaces are not thought of as places for recreation, inner-block parks acquire an association with backstage functions; that is, with things nor-

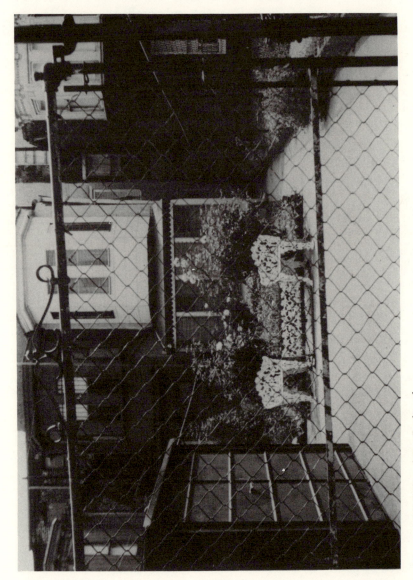

30 A Well-Cared-For Backyard

Fenced, paved and planted, but seldom used. Photograph by the author.

mally kept out of public view. If residents have trash they want to dispose of and they do not know (or care to know) the established procedures, the park in the back is a logical and convenient dumping place. Because the park is not associated with any one house, the Health Inspector cannot determine which residents are responsible for the dumping. Residents are seldom able to identify the offenders; they usually put the blame on "outsiders". The association of park with backstage functions is reinforced by the fact that abutting houses are required to put their trash in the alley to await collection, and by the time the garbage truck comes a good deal of trash has found its way into the park.

The fact that the inner-block parks are at the back and hidden from public view makes them an attractive place for individuals and groups who want to be out of the public eye: winos, kids playing hooky from school, people using and pushing drugs. This is the reason why some residents stay out of the parks, and why they tell their children not to play there.

The situation is quite different in a middle-income area. Here the back yards are seen as an extension of the living space; they are used for relaxation and entertaining and furnished with brick paving, flowerbeds, garden chairs, and umbrellas. Decks are built and residents open up their houses with picture windows and french doors. Walls, fences, and hedges screen the yard from view. When residents want to "sit out" they go to the back.

PARKS

The parks are used well below capacity. To some extent this is because people want to be on the streetfront, but it is also because people do not want to be in the parks.

Some problems are inherent in the nature of the facility. Parks concentrate play in a single place, and in doing so they increase opportunities for conflict. Children fight over the use of the swings, they get pushed off the climbers, and threatened by bullies; undesirable people and strangers from other neighborhoods (houses on two sides of an inner-block park are sometimes considered to be in different neighborhoods) set a bad example and they are rough; teenagers "take over" the park. Many parents feel that children are more likely to be hurt in a park than anywhere else.

These problems are aggravated by the parks' location and by the poor fit between design and use. The inner-block location means that the parks are hidden from public view and, because of the way back spaces are perceived in the community, from neighborhood consciousness: there is inadequate surveillance, and children get cut on broken glass. Parents prefer their children to play on the streetfront where they can keep an eye on them.

Parks are seldom used by those for whom they were designed, or for purposes and in ways that were intended. This is a source of frequent complaint. Parents complain about the fact that the play equipment is not being used as it was meant to be. Part of the trouble is that the parks serve essentially the same

31   Playing Ball in the Park

Ball games are staged in between the play equipment. Photograph courtesy of Baltimore City Department of Planning.

children on a continuing basis, children who are there less because of the park's special amenities than because of its location—it is near home. Using the playground day after day, they soon master the challenge of the equipment, but the equipment does not go away when it ceases to be fun—it remains there, fixed and permanent. So the children look for other things to do on it. They twist the chains so that the swings spin around, play chase along the monkey-bars, and balance on the backs of benches. Then they play ball in the spaces in between the pieces of equipment.

Many of the games that children play regularly are not included in the design program for the parks. These games are part of the play culture of the neighborhood, being passed down from one generation to another. The rules are widely known, sometimes with small differences between one block to another. The games do not require outside organization or supervision; use the steps, walls, surfaces and spaces commonly found in the neighborhood rather than special courts; accommodate themselves to a wide range of settings; and can be played without special equipment. They take place in the street, sidewalk, alley, or yard, but as a rule they are not contained by any one of these spaces. When the parks became a part of the network of neighborhood play spaces, they started to be used for traditional games even though they had not been designed for them. The parks are often used for ball games because ball playing is popular, and because the parks are the most suitable spaces available, even if the equipment gets in the way and despite the "No Ball Playing" signs. Traditional games leave traces in the form of numbers and signs, in paint and chalk, on vertical and horizontal surfaces and on equipment. From these traces and from discussions with local children it is possible, therefore, to trace the lines of the *as-used* parks. These bear little relationship either to the equipment or to the spatial divisions or levels of the *as-designed* parks (see Fig. 10.1).

The pattern of use of the parks does not fit with generally accepted design concepts. Most parks are divided into subareas, each intended for a particular user group and furnished for a particular type of activity: there are areas for use by adults (seats and game tables), toddlers (small equipment), young children (larger equipment), and, in the case of only one park, teenagers (basketball). In fact, however, the separation between age groups who use the parks is often temporal rather than spatial: young children use the park—all of it—in the morning, older children take over in the afternoons, and teenagers and young adults take over in the evenings. None of the groups pay much attention to the division into activity areas.

The lack of fit between park design and park use reflects the unrealistic expectations of the park designers—the residents who write the program as well as the professionals who carry it out. They take the attitude that prevailing social behavior is undesirable, but to allow it to influence the design solution is to accept it as a legitimate foundation for the future. One has to have faith that conditions will improve, and one has to design for things as they should be, not as they are. This kind of reasoning explains why residents can insist on the need

32 Traces of Play in the Park

A wall in the park shows markings associated with ball games. Photograph by the author.

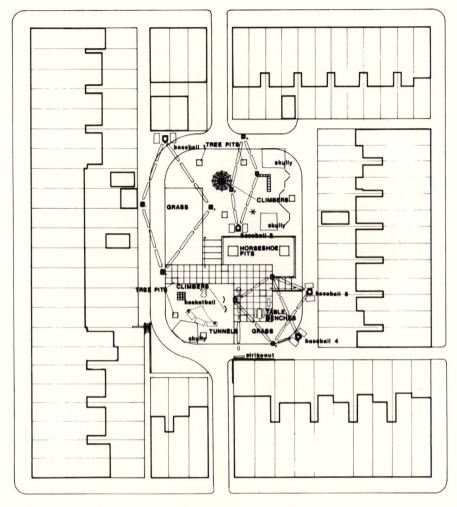

Figure 10.1   Parks As-Designed and As-Used

One of the parks as it was designed and as it was used. There were few points of relationship between the two arrangements. Illustration courtesy of Baltimore City Department of Planning.

for play equipment while maintaining that they do not permit their own children to play in the parks, or why they ask for benches for elderly people even though they know that elderly people seldom venture into the parks. What residents really want are conditions under which children *will* be playing in the park and elderly people *will* feel safe enough to sit there, and so that is what they design for. There is a general belief that ongoing behavior will change to conform to a desirable physical environment.

Residents are also somewhat unrealistic in the kinds of activities they call for. They design "passive" parks and they are disappointed when (as they might have anticipated) the users are highly active. They make virtually no provision for teenagers, who are felt to be noisy, undisciplined, and dangerous, and then they are dismayed when teenagers use the parks. Parents ask for things they would *like* their children to do rather than things that they *do* do. Residents whose houses abut the park are more concerned with minimizing nuisance than with satisfying recreational needs (make no mistake, living against a park can be very unpleasant) and some of them want the park to be a quiet garden, although such a facility could not survive conditions of public access, low maintenance, and high population density. Others see the park as a way of getting the city to assume responsibility for a vacant, unsanitary parcel of land, and they are disappointed when the level of maintenance and policing are inadequate to put an end to vandalism and littering.

In ignoring existing behaviors, both residents and professionals fail to anticipate the problems that are likely to arise, and do nothing to minimize the opportunities for disruption, or to make the parks easier to control.

NEAR-HOME SPACES

Places immediately around the home—street, sidewalk, alley, yard, and park—are places people feel most responsible for, and where they feel safest and most in control. These places are essentially an extension of home, and they provide a network of play places that encompasses the entire block.

For children, play is an intimate part of daily life. Children have detailed knowledge of the play opportunities and challenges of all near-home spaces and the surfaces and objects in them. Boys like spaces that are large, clear, and level for games; hard surfaces for ball playing and soft surfaces for wrestling; and slopes, hills, and curves for riding bicycles and skating. They like private places and places for watching games and sports, walking, climbing, and balancing. Girls like places with lots of space for running and playing games. They like shade, places to sit and talk, skipping, music, bands, and parties.

Children are familiar with a great many traditional games, such as duck-duck goose, two squares, all'y-all'y-in-free, step-back-Sally, "its", bank robbers, jacks, tin-can-alley, follow-the leader, skelly, and stickball (see Robinson and Associates, 1977). These games spill out over all near-home spaces. Alleys and sidewalks are good for linear games involving balls, bicycles, and skates; yards and the vestibules of houses are good for hiding, electric light poles are good for climbing, fences for scaling, fire escapes for sitting, steps for sitting and playing step ball, walls for playing strikeout. The lines on the sidewalks are good for playing four-squares, and hilly streets are good for wheeled toys, bicycling, and skating.

Young children are generally not allowed to cross the street by themselves, and so their play is confined to the block (although it must be said that children

33   Play in Near-Home Spaces

Four Squares can be played on any hard, smooth surface. It requires a large rubber ball, and five or more players. The court is divided into four squares. (When played on the sidewalk, the game uses the scored lines in the pavement.) One player stands next to each square facing inward. Waiting players form a line. One square is for the server or "king". The server bounces the ball on the server square and then punches it into one of the other three squares. The player on that square punches the ball onto another square, and the game continues in this fashion until a player misses the ball or allows it to go out of bounds. That player is out, and goes to the end of the waiting line. Each of the other three players moves up one square and a new player from the front of the line moves to the empty square. Photograph courtesy of Baltimore City Department of Planning.

do not necessarily do what they are told). Their play is frequently interrupted by visits home for comforting, refreshment, rest, and to use the bathroom. Children also like to be near home so that they can call on their parents for help, often because they feel threatened by older children, and parents respond by coming out and scolding the bullies or complaining to their parents.

Older children are permitted to stray farther from home (and some of them get involved in things that would horrify their parents if they knew) but they still spend most of their time close to home. Strange neighborhoods are seen, especially by the boys, as places for adventuring. Parks are high on their list of play places, but streets and sidewalks, stores (especially those where the attendants are friendly and the goods are affordable), churches, community facilities (the bathroom in the firehouse is a great convenience), school grounds, and

34   Play in Near-Home Spaces

Skelly (also called skully) is played by two to six players, on a square court between twelve and eighteen feet to a side, that is drawn on a level, preferably smooth surface. Usually the court is marked in chalk on the pavement of a street or playground. The court contains numbered boxes (thirteen is common, but there may be as many as thirty), the highest number being the central box. Each player has a token (usually a weighted bottlecap) and the game is to shoot or flick one's token from one box to another in ascending order until one reaches the central box, and then in descending order until one returns to the first box. If the token falls outside a box, or on a line, the player forfeits a turn and the next player has a chance. If the token accidentally lands in the central square, it must remain there until it is knocked out. The first one to complete the entire sequence wins the game. Photograph courtesy of Baltimore City Department of Planning.

houses of friends are often more fun. Many play activities involve interactions with the adult world—selling, running errands, conversing, visiting, buying, even playing games.

Parents and children are both very much aware of the danger of automobile traffic, but many children are specifically told to play on the streetfront because mothers can more easily keep an eye on them there, because of fighting on the playground, and because children hurt themselves on the equipment.

It is not only children who stay close to home. Adults spend most of their recreational time in the immediate vicinity of home. They choose spaces not so much for their intrinsic qualities as for their location: they are close to home. Much of adults' recreational time consists of time taken in between household chores, and being close to home means that they can still listen out for the telephone or the baby, attend to the front door, and keep an eye on the stove

35   Play in Near-Home Spaces

Children recognize play potential and challenge in everyday objects whether or not these objects are "meant" for play. Photograph courtesy of Baltimore City Department of Planning.

36   Play in Near-Home Spaces

Step ball is usually played in the street and sidewalk, against the hard steps of a rowhouse. One player, the "bouncer", bounces the ball against the steps so that it ricochets back towards the other players who jump for the ball. A player who catches the ball with one hand becomes the new bouncer. A player who catches the ball with two hands must catch the ball a second time with the same bouncer at the "mound". A game may continue for hours as new players join in and old ones drop out. Photograph courtesy of Baltimore City Department of Planning.

37   Play in Near-Home Spaces

Strikeout is played against a solid wall, preferably not less than eight feet high. A strike zone, about 24 inches square and 20 to 30 inches off the ground, is drawn on the wall. The game is played by two teams (it can be played by as few as two people), one at bat and the other in the field. The pitcher aims the ball at the square on the wall—inside the square is a "strike," outside is a "ball." There is one pitcher for each batter. The batter tries for a hit or home run. A swing and miss is a strike, three strikes are an out, four balls a walk. After three outs, the batting team takes to the field. Photograph courtesy of Baltimore City Department of Planning.

155

Much of the recreational activity that takes place is, then, home-based in the sense that it is unlikely it can be diverted to a park no matter how well designed. People use near-home spaces because they are nearby, convenient, accessible, and because people see them as an extension of home.

COMMUNITY RESPONSIBILITIES

Most of the problems in the parks stem from uncivil behavior. The City does not have the resources to adequately manage the parks; the most it can offer is to provide a regular trash pickup. The original plan for Harlem Park assumed that people who lived around a park would take a special interest in it and join together in order to look after it. But resident-management is not easy to achieve, and the job of management is made harder because of the way the parks were designed and located.

Community has a spatial component. In Harlem Park, neighbors see the street as the locus of common interests. If we think of a city block as the area bounded by four streets, then most of the people that residents know on the block live on their street; and they are more likely to form friendships, exchange childcare services, share club memberships, borrow things from and lend things to people who live on their street. In fact for residents, the street with its houses on both sides *is* the block; people who live on the same street block are a community and people who live around the corner, even if they back against a common alley or park, are a different community. One can expect members of a community to feel a collective responsibility for facilities that lie within their boundaries and so one would expect Harlem Park residents to feel a collective responsibility for the sidewalk in their block, but not necessarily for the park at the back. This expectation is confirmed by the fact that residents regularly sweep and wash the sidewalks, but they do very little to improve the condition of the parks.

There are several explanations as to why residents looked after the sidewalks. I have mentioned one: the sidewalks fall within the boundaries of "natural" communities. Another explanation is that residents have a legal obligation to keep the sidewalks clean and unobstructed: the City had the right to issue a citation to any resident who allows trash to collect in front of the house. But residents go beyond the legal requirements. They put out plants and furniture, some even paint the pavement. They take a proprietary attitude towards the space, and they watch over it and use it as an extension of home. Even though it is public space, the special rights of residents are generally recognized and accepted. Outsiders may move along the sidewalk, but they have no right to "hang around" like residents and if they do, residents feel they have a right to object: they intervene directly, or they call the police and complain about suspicious persons or loitering. This combination of responsibility and privilege explains residents' involvement in managing the streetfront.

Conditions in the parks are quite different. Planners and designers describe

38   Residents Take Responsibility for the Sidewalk

The front of the house is the face that residents present to the public. Residents are far more likely to feel responsible for the condition of the front than the back. Photograph courtesy of Baltimore City Department of Planning.

the parks as being in the center of the block, but as residents see it, *inter*-block parks is a more accurate description because they are located at the junction of four different street blocks and not clearly within the jurisdiction of any one block group. There is also no legal requirement for residents to care for the parks. Residents see park maintenance as a City responsibility; they see their own responsibility as limited to keeping an eye on things and calling the City when they see something that needs attention. The parks are open to the public at all times and there are no clear rules as to what might or might not be done there. (There are "No Ball Playing" and "No Dumping" signs, but these can be ignored with impunity, and so they have no currency.)

In a facility where the activity has a recognizable structure and form, such as a game court, it is easy to tell whether it is being properly used, but is a man sitting on the park bench recreating or loitering? Are teenagers huddled in the shelter just chatting, or are they waiting for you to leave so that they can break into your house? One cannot tell proper use by looking, and this makes it difficult to know when to intervene. In any case, intervention would probably be ineffectual because abutting residents do not have privileged use of the parks as they do of the sidewalks, and attempts to regulate activities are resented and challenged; they can be dangerous. Calling the police does not help because there are so

39   Residents Have Special Rights Over the Sidewalk

Residents exercise privileged use of the sidewalk in front of their home. They furnish it as if it were private space. Outsiders may move through, but lingerers invites suspicion. Photograph courtesy of Baltimore City Department of Planning.

40   "No Ball Playing" Sign in the Park

Signs do not mean anything unless they are backed up with action. Photograph courtesy of Baltimore City Department of Planning.

many entrances to the parks that offenders can easily escape by one entrance while the police are coming in at another. To add to these problems, the parks, unlike the sidewalk, do not lend themselves to being parcelled off so that responsibility automatically falls to individual residents; a park is a single parcel and it requires coordinated rather than parallel action. This, in turn, requires an effective, structured community organization, something that does not come easily to residents of Harlem Park.

In the absence of the City and of local residents, no one manages the parks. The result would not have been quite as bad if residents were prepared to accept the prevalent pattern of behavior, but residents see the parks as a step toward changing behavior, and the physical facilities by themselves are not able to accomplish this.

THE VALUE OF RESEARCH

Residents have little faith in the general value of research. They want to improve local conditions, but they do not believe in universal solutions. Residents do not see their neighborhood as a prototype, but as a place unlike any other. It has its own unique history, its residents are people and not representatives of any population group, and its leaders are individuals, each with his or her own special strengths, weaknesses, sympathies, ties and rivalries. Things happen because of the actions of specific people and not because of general rules. If a program is to be successful in the neighborhood it is because local people are determined that it will work, and not because it had been found to work elsewhere. And if it has worked elsewhere that does not mean that it will work here: there is little to be learned from the experiences of other people in other places. The only way to find out if it will work here is to try it here.

Nor do residents take kindly to the idea that all aspects of research—posing hypotheses, identifying information to be collected, developing instruments for collecting the information, doing analysis, and drawing conclusions—will be controlled by outsiders: the researchers may say that they are evaluating a program, but actually they are evaluating the residents. The fact that the researchers are scientists only makes matters worse, because they cannot be relied on to have the "right attitudes." Community leaders are more concerned about the researchers' attitudes than about their professional competence; they would much prefer the researchers to be advocates rather than examiners. Who needs research anyway? If anyone wants to know whether things are working in the neighborhood and if not why not, one has only to ask the residents.

11

Design Guidelines

Guidelines are based on the conclusions of the studies, and are intended as guides for future planning and design in Harlem Park and in similar neighborhoods.

1. Keep the Streetfront Alive

Maintain active use of the streetfront. There is some loss of privacy, but this is the price one has to pay for security.

Residents should be able to watch over the street. This means that there should be windows and frequent points of access. Devices such as grilles and painted screens should be used to increase privacy (Eff, 1984). Bay windows are useful in that they give view down the street as well as across it.

Eliminate dead spaces by making sure that every space is useful, accessible and visible. Small units with many entrances along the street are preferred to large multi-unit structures with one common entrance. In apartment buildings, each ground floor unit should have its own entrance off the street.

2. Encourage Residents to Use the Streetfront

Recognize that the feeling of security on the streetfront is associated not just with the presence of people, but with the presence of *other residents*—people who know one another, who have a social investment in the area, and who are likely to help one another in time of need.

The City should encourage features of the streetfront that attract *residents* to use it. There should be room for residents to sit outside the stream of pedestrian

Figure 11.1   Use of Window Screens for Privacy

Painted window screens are used in some Baltimore row-house neighborhoods to increase privacy. A picture is painted on the outside surface of the mesh. The paint does not block the holes so that from the inside one has an unobstructed view out, but from the outside one's eyes are confused by the picture and one cannot see in. Illustration by the author.

traffic. Street hawkers should be encouraged. Mobile units should be utilized for delivering city services. Baltimore has, over the years, used many mobile units to bring city services out into the neighborhoods; they include the Fun Wagon, Crafts Wagon, Skatemobile, Sidewalk Theater, Bookmobile, Mobile Health Screening Unit, Fire Prevention Bus, Officer Friendly Van, Talking Traffic Light, and Timmy The Talking Trashcan.

3. Recognize Recreation as a Legitimate Use of the Sidewalk

Design sidewalks to accommodate sitting-out and play because, whether planned for or not, the sidewalk is the place where most home-based recreation is going to happen.

Sidewalks should not, however, be designed so that they "read" as a park or a playground because this would disrupt the behavior-control mechanism that operates on the streetfront but not in a park. Closing the street to traffic and

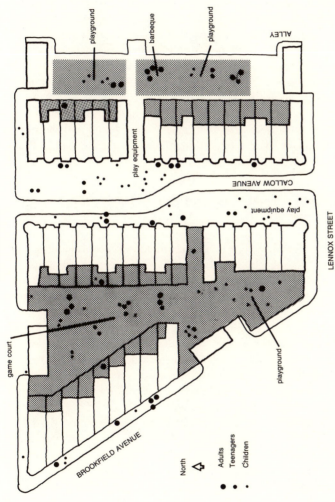

Figure 11.2   Callow Avenue: Home-Based Recreation Taken into Account in Design

Peter D. Paul, Architects, applied the findings of the study in their design for renovating a block of row houses in the study area. The architects proposed that the triangular parcel of land in the back be fenced in to eliminate direct public access. The architects also recommended that the street be redesigned so as to reduce traffic speed and volume, and accommodate increased recreational use. Symbols show the anticipated distribution of recreators. The completed project is very much like the original design. It is run as a co-operative and functions successfully. Illustration by the author.

furnishing it with benches and play equipment would attract outsiders into the area and send the message that play is a right and not a privilege, and this would remove residents' authority to stop play when it became a nuisance. The approach, then, should not be to create a recreational area, but to create a streetfront that is pleasant and safe for recreational use. Pavement and steps should be made suitable for sitting and playing, steps should be strong enough for stepball, walls for stickball. Windows should be protected against stray balls. Where possible, covered porches should be provided for protection in inclement weather. There should be good surveillance from each unit and easy access from the unit to the street. Residents should be able to bring out their own seats and play equipment and remove it or protect it from unauthorized use. (A common custom in Baltimore is to tip up the seat when it is not in use.)

The design objective is not to eliminate nuisance but rather to maximize residents' ability to deal with nuisances that arise. The sidewalk will be noisy and this is a cost of living in an area like Harlem Park. Accumulation of litter should be reduced by making sure that adequate trash cans are provided.

4. Cut Down on the Speed and Volume of Automobile Traffic

Reduce volume and speed of through traffic on residential streets.

Intense traffic reduces livability. The nuisance caused by noise and fumes, and the high accident rate among children has been well documented (see, for example, Appleyard 1981). The impact of automobile traffic is especially severe because of the high density, large number of children, and the active use of the streetfront.

Where through traffic cannot be rerouted, the street might be closed during certain periods of the day, using portable barricades; or traffic might be slowed down by means of devices such as a neck in the road at the entrances to the block, or a road surface that causes discomfort when drivers exceed the posted speed limit. Residential streets should be made to look different from through streets by using a distinctively different pavement.

The traffic-free pedestrian street and the dead-end street are not desirable solutions. Automobile traffic brings additional lights at night and patrolling police cars. A through street also generates more activity along the front, and it makes sure that you will not be "cornered"; that you will always have a way of getting away in an emergency.

5. Buildings Must Not Turn Their Backs on the Street

The Radburn principle, where the buildings are arranged in a superblock with pedestrian access from the inside, is not appropriate here.

In a typical Radburn type of layout, parking lots are located along the streetfront, and the housing units take their access from a system of private

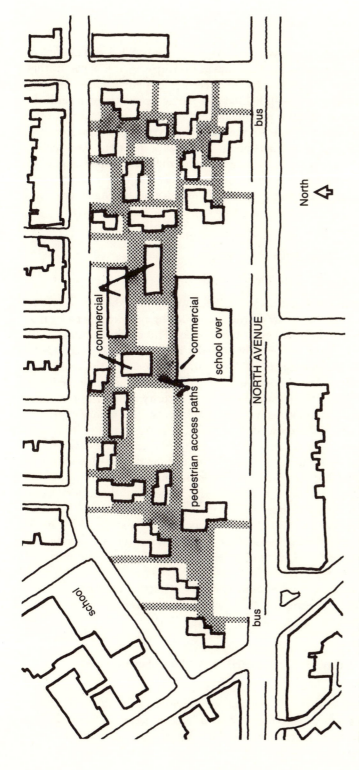

Figure 11.3 A Radburn Type of Layout in the Study Area

A project in the study area, completed in the early 1970's, contains walk-up apartments, a school and a small shopping center. The school and the stores lead off an interior plaza which is not visible from the street. Paths link the plaza with the surrounding streets and connect to an interior path system that provides access to the apartments. The paths also provide non-project residents with a shortcut to the stores, the school, and the bus. Parking lots separate the housing from the streets. The design brings outsiders through the back spaces and removes residents from the streets. It violates the conventions that contribute to the security of both back and front spaces. Illustration by the author.

walkways along which, at scattered locations, there are benches and clusters of play equipment. If one regards the walkways as front spaces, it is apparent that they do not have as much opportunity for street life as a public street, nor will they be as well policed and as well lighted as a public street. If one regards the walkways as back spaces, then they provide outsiders with ready access to the back (the problem is especially acute if the walkways serve as a shortcut from one part of the neighborhood to another) and raise a host of questions about public and private rights; for example, is the equipment for the use of residents only? In addition, the public street will become less safe because residents no longer offer surveillance there, and there will be increased reliance on the vigilance of the police.

6. Keep Outsiders Away from Back Spaces

Back spaces should not be accessible to outsiders.

Designers sometimes feel that to get the back spaces safer they should try to duplicate the active life that exists on the streetfront by encouraging pedestrian movement through the alleys and inner-block parks. This can be a mistake. The possibility for pedestrian movement through the back spaces, by itself, is unlikely to change the prevalent pattern of front-use, especially if the units have their access of the front. The opportunity for outsiders to pass through the inner-block spaces is not likely to increase the sense of security; it may, in fact, have the opposite effect, unless abutting residents can be persuaded to take a proprietary interest in the back space the same as they currently do in the front.

A more dependable approach would be to restrict access to the back spaces. Eliminate direct access from the street, and restrict use of the back spaces to surrounding residents and their guests. This is the most direct way of placing control of the space in the hands of the residents. This means that utility access to the units must be provided from the front.

An alternative would be to restrict access to the interior spaces only at certain times, for example by closing them up at night. This requires a community organization to enforce. Who evicts outsiders at dusk? Who locks the gates and opens them up again in the morning?

Security in the back can be further increased by attracting residents to use it. Either for recreation or there may be other more practical applications, like washing the car, parking.

7. Increase the Recreational Potential of All Neighborhood Spaces

Home-based recreation—that is, recreational activities tied to domestic chores and responsibilities—must be recognized as a basic function of housing, and provision for home-based recreation must be made in all housing plans.

This does not necessarily mean that all recreation must be accommodated on private property, or in special recreational facilities. The recreational potential of all near-home spaces should be considered and they should be designed to increase their recreational potential. In considering each space, designers should ask, "What is this space likely to be used for, what can I do to facilitate or discourage this use, and what would be the most effective way of doing it?"

Many of these near-home spaces compete with parks and playgrounds as places for recreation. A roller skating rink in a park, for example, may have a difficult time attracting kids off a hilly city street; a park bench may be deserted because people prefer to sit on their front steps, or the bench may land up in the middle of a ball game because there is not a better near-home space for playing ball. If the playground cannot be made more attractive than its competition, then energy might be better spent making the non-park spaces safer. In introducing new recreational facilities, thought should be given to its probable effect on the existing environment: will it replace certain elements (will climbing equipment replace fences as places for climbing), will it shift activities elsewhere (will ball games be played on the playfield in future rather than the street), or will it extend them?

Spaces should not be considered independently, but as a linked system that winds around and between houses. Designers who concern themselves only with parks ignore the places where people spend most of their recreational time. A plan for improving the quality of the residential environment must be concerned with improving recreational opportunities in the neighborhood, not just with the design of parks.

8. Make Parks Attractive to Adult Users

Design parks so that they attract adults to recreate there, because adult recreators provide supervision for young children. One cannot, however, attract adults by appealing to their sense of civic responsibility; the only way to attract them is to make it enjoyable for them to be there.

This means that adults should be able to participate in the play activity and that there should be a role for them in facilitating childrens' play. There is a strong tendency to fill playgrounds with play equipment. The function of the equipment is to replace a play leader, and adults are reduced to the passive and thankless job of watching, cautioning, and reprimanding. The alternative approach is to design parks so that adults are *necessary* in order to facilitate play activities, that their presence contributes to rather than inhibits the quality of the play experience.

This could mean providing shelter, benches, and tables for adults to sit and talk or to run arts and crafts programs for children, ball fields where adults can participate in the game with children, sprinklers that can be switched on and off by means of a key which is kept by an abutting resident; night lights that can be similarly controlled by local residents; movable seating and equipment that can be taken out when needed and then returned; nets and balls in charge of local residents to be given out at scheduled times and removed at others. In all of these examples, the children depend on the presence of the adult for play opportunity, and in addition, the adults have control so that if play becomes a nuisance, it can be terminated. It also means that when the adult is not there to supervise, the activity stops.

9. Design Parks for a Variety of Contingencies

Play activity will depend less on the designers' intentions than on what the players think the space is "good" for. Activities that are not part of the local play culture will not occur no matter what the playground is "designed for," and a popular play activity will occur in feasible places without regard for the designers' intentions.

No landscape is so specialized that it is suitable only for one kind of play and no popular games so rigid that they cannot be adapted to a variety of landscapes. The designer should ask, What is likely to happen here if the uses I am planning for *do not* happen?

The most suitable kind of playground is one that can be compared to the stage of a theater that has no fixed set, but that is far more than bare boards; it is equipped to accommodate a succession of changing performances. Where the use of a space cannot be controlled and cannot be predicted with accuracy, it is necessary to provide for a number of contingencies. This suggests such things as sleeves for securing posts, hookups for lighting, power, and sound, water connections, lighting that can be regulated, equipment that can be moved, access to toilets and storage space, and provisions for delivery, erection, and removal of temporary equipment and structures. Equipment should be selected that allows for a wide range of uses: benches and tables may be intended for game playing, but they can also be used for crab feasts, arts and crafts classes, or simply sitting around. In the same way, a high wall could be intended as a screen, but it could be used for a game of strikeout, for murals or graffitti, to climb over, or to project a movie onto. Steps can be used for coin-pitching games, for playing stepball, or for sitting and playing "jacks". A low railing used to separate one activity area from another can also make do as a "net" in a game of volleyball and so join the two spaces; or it can be used for sitting or balancing on. A hardtop surface can be used for a variety of court games depending on its size; but it can also be used for riding bicycles, and if it is on an incline it is good for wheeled toys and roller-skating. A patch of dirt can be used for digging or for planting. A pole can be used for scaling or for fixing a basketball net. Spaces can be designed so that each subarea and piece of equipment is suitable not simply for a single designated use, but for the most likely acceptable alternatives, including adult activities such as carwashing and community meetings, leaving it to the users to settle on those that are the most desirable, or least objectionable.

In an area such as Harlem Park, varying conflicting groups vie with one another for the use of the space, and the many problems associated with the facility will not be decided by having specialized play equipment. It will only be decided by the management, and children's play equipment does not offer enough incentive or sufficient reward to develop management skills among residents, nor does it provide the management group with sufficient flexibility to negotiate with potential user groups.

10. Do Not Put Active Parks Hard Against Houses

Near-home spaces are best for home-based recreation. Parks are noisy, untidy, they attract outsiders, are used at all hours of the day and night, and can be very unpleasant to live next to.

For these reasons, parks intended for intensive use should not be put hard against houses, and parks hard against houses should not be designed for intensive use. Parks on small, tight parcels of land are best if they cater only to immediate residents and do not attract outsiders. This is especially true of parks in back spaces. They should, in fact, be designed to exclude outsiders, and intensity of use should not be used as a measure of success.

Facilities for intensive use should be placed where they can be buffered from the adjacent houses—across a street, for example.

11. Every Space Must Belong to Somebody

Every outdoor space must be designed as an occupancy by a particular person or community, or the public; that is, there must be someone who has say over its use and responsibility for its ongoing use and upkeep.

The elements of an occupancy include the presence of a willing individual, organization or agency, an ability to accept the responsibilities associated with primary occupancy of the space, and the right to exercise control over it. There must be no left over or unassigned spaces. (For a discussion of occupancy types, see pp. 67–72.)

In the case of public spaces, responsibility must be assigned to a specific agency. Too often, management responsibilities are divided among various departments—one for keeping it clean, one for keeping it safe, one for making repairs, and so on—but no single department has overall responsibility. Public spaces must have a supervisor for the times that they are open to the public; at the very least, someone who fulfills the same function as a lifeguard at a swimming pool: to be responsible for enforcing the rules, to give assistance in case of need, and to put a stop to activities that could be harmful. Special attention must be paid to the security of these spaces at night. This may mean special lighting and policing. The most effective way of dealing with this problem is to restrict public access to the space either permanently or during the most trouble-prone time (usually at night). This means that fences and gates must be provided at all public access points. To keep the load manageable, the spaces must be visible from public streets.

If public resources are inadequate to provide proper management, then one must look into the possibility of assigning the space (through transfer of ownership, lease, or informal arrangement) to an organization such as a church group, cooperative, club, or community association. The organization should be one that is established and has a history of successful accomplishment. Alternatively, one might consider assigning the space to a developer as part of a housing or housing-related package, or to an individual householder for private use. Combination-occupancies are also possible. For example, the City could offer an organization money, services, or rights in return for public access; and a community group could assign portions of its space to individual members for their own use and maintenance. In partnership cases, it is important that the privileges and responsibilities of each partner be clearly spelled out.

As one goes from general occupancy to community occupancy to personal occupancy (for an explanation of these terms see Chapter 5), the degree of public control over the use of the facility is diminished, and so one must be prepared to accept the fact that instead of a public park one may get a parking lot, a day care center, community gardens, or extensions of private yards. In all cases, an attempt should be made to create an environment in which the occupant's efforts are rewarded and the demands upon individuals are kept to a minimum. The space should be fully visible and directly accessible to the occupants. Abutting houses should have windows that look over the space and, if possible, entrances that lead from it. Entrances for the general public should be clearly defined and kept to a minimum. Designs should be such as to clearly discourage users that the managing group wishes to exclude. This may mean adding illumination at night, opening views, changing floor levels, introducing physical obstructions, and eliminating equipment.

It is as important to design for the inhibition of undesirable uses as for the accommodation of desirable ones. Special facilities and equipment that are not available elsewhere can be a powerful attraction for outsiders, and add greatly to management problems.

In all cases, the use of each space must be compatible with the type of occupancy. Where management resources are relatively small and the chances of challenge are relatively great, the design of each space must be examined for the demands it places on management, the extent to which it supports management, and the opportunities it presents for building management skills. Spaces must have a design and a system of management that are most appropriate for their situation, taking into account the structure and strength of the community, the nature of prevailing conditions in the neighborhood, the constraints of the site, and the activities that are wanted in the space.

12. Help Residents to Manage Neighborhood Spaces

Residents cannot be expected to manage community open spaces without help in the form of cash, materials, services, encouragement, and/or recognition.

It may take the form of trash removal, code inspection and enforcement, repair and replacement of equipment, workshops in play leadership and plant care, provision of brooms, spades, mowers, clippers, paint, plants, mulch, arts-and-crafts supplies, and trashbags, training officials in City departments to deal with community complaints, arranging for exchange of information between various community management groups, providing media coverage of community events, offering official recognition for the contribution made by community volunteers, and arranging a competition with prizes for the best-managed blocks. One of the keys to success is to make community management fun.

In order to provide this kind of assistance, the City must recognize that a commitment of resources is the price for relinquishing sole responsibility for the management of community open spaces. The City must employ environmental managers, people who are skillful in handling interpersonal and interdepartmental relations, management, behavior analysis, and creative design. The environmental managers must coordinate public and private plans for the location, design, and management of new open spaces. They must work with design professionals and public officials who are involved in the design of new open spaces, providing them with information about the social ecology of the community in which the facility is located. They must meet with residents who are involved in planning new open spaces, and tell them of problems that other residents have had with similar spaces elsewhere, and discuss the likelihood that similar problems might occur in this neighborhood. They must conduct post-occupancy evaluations of open spaces and use the findings to develop and refine design guidelines and standards. They must be able to coordinate resident-run and City services, negotiate with residents to take over certain management functions in exchange for others (for example, sweeping the inner-block park in exchange for more frequent trash pick-up). They should arrange for household garbage to be collected in the fronts in blocks that have inner-block parks. They should see that City departments respond promptly to complaints by community-management groups. They should review applications for temporary street-closings for recreation programs and festivals.

In some cases increased community involvement will result in cost savings as management functions are shifted to local residents. In other cases, however, community management may mean an increase in city services. In any event it will mean a restructuring of public recreation programs with greater emphasis on portable equipment, a library-like system for lending out equipment, and recruiting and training local residents as recreation leaders.

13. Help Residents Solve a Design Problem. Don't Solve It for Them

Designers should see their role as helping residents to solve their problems, rather than solving problems for them.

This means a readiness to hand over design decisions to the local residents. It does not mean the professional designer relinquishes responsibility for the design, but rather that he plays the role of an advisor, helping in the formulation of the design program, translating residents' needs into design solutions, spelling out the implications of alternative solutions, and recommending those that have the greatest chance for success. Because resident management is so important to the success of any facility, designers must take a *process*-directed rather than a *product*-directed approach, seeing the final outcome not as a blueprint, but rather as a process through which to develop a sense of community and strengthen management skills. Designers must help to develop an organization that is able to devise, test, fine-tune, and revise activities that are associated with the continuing operation of the space. Designers are successful if the residents take credit for the performance of the facility.

This is a new role for designers, one that is not defined by custom, and it requires them to do things that they are not trained for. The tendency to "design it, build it, and leave it," must give way to a process in which design development, testing, and modification can continue through a period during which the facility is in use.

Bibliography

Aldskogins, H. A conceptual framework and a Swedish case study of recreational behavior and environmental cognition. *Economic Geography* 53 (April 2, 1977): 163–83.

Allen, Lady Marjorie, of Hurtwood. *Planning for Play*. Cambridge, MA: MIT Press, 1968.

Appleyard, D. Home. *Architectural Association Quarterly* 11 no. 3 (1979a): 4–20.

———. Inside vs. outside: the distortions of distance. Berkeley, CA: Institute of Urban and Regional Development, University of California, Berkeley, working paper no. 307 (July 1979b).

———. *Planning a Pluralist City*. Cambridge, MA: MIT Press, 1976.

———. Motion, sequence, and the city. In G. Kepes (ed.), *The Nature and Art of Motion*. New York: George Braziller, 1965.

Appleyard, D., and K. Craik. The Berkeley environmental simulation laboratory: its use in environmental impact assessment. In T. Dickert and K. Domeny (eds.), *Environmental Impact Assessment*. Berkeley, CA: University of California Press, 1974.

Appleyard, D., with M. S. Gerson and M. Lintell. *Livable Streets*. Berkeley, CA: University of California Press, 1981.

Ashihara, Y. *The Aesthetic Townscape*. Cambridge, MA: MIT Press, 1983.

Bacon, E. N. *Design of Cities*. New York: Viking, 1967.

Baltimore City Department of Planning. Neighborhood design study: progress report no. 1. Baltimore, MD (December 1971).

———. Neighborhood design study: progress report no. 2. Baltimore, MD (April 1972).

———. Neighborhood design study: progress report no. 3. Baltimore, MD (August 1973).

———. *A Year of Celebration*. (Report to the National Endowment for the Arts, Washington, D.C.) Baltimore, MD (1977).

174   Bibliography

Barker, R. G. Behavior settings: human habitats and behavior machines. In Roger G. Barker and Associates (eds.), *Habitats, Environments and Human Behavior.* San Francisco, CA: Jossey-Bass, 1978, pp. 192–201.

Barker, R. G., and H. F. Wright. *One Boy's Day.* New York: Harper and Row, 1951.

Baumer, T., and A. Hunter. Perceived street traffic, social integration and fear of crime. Evanston IL: Northwestern University, Center for Urban Affairs, June 1979.

Becker, H. Do photographs tell the truth? *Afterimage* (February 1978): 9–13.

————. Photography and sociology. *Studies in the Anthropology of Visual Communication,* 1 no. 1 (Fall 1974): 3–26.

Berger, J. *Ways of Seeing.* New York: Penguin, 1977.

Birch, D. L., E. S. Brown, R. P. Coleman, D. W. Da Lomba, W. L. Parsons, L. C. Sharpe, and S. A. Weber. *The Behavioral Foundations of Neighborhood Change.* Cambridge, MA: Joint Center for Urban Studies of the MIT and Harvard University, March 1977.

Balke, B. F., K. Weigl, and R. Perloff. Perceptions of the ideal community. *Journal of Applied Psychology,* 60 no. 5 (1975): 612–15.

Boorstin, D. *The Image: A Guide to Pseudo Events in America.* New York: Harper and Row, 1961.

Bosselman, F. P. *In the Wake of the Tourist: Managing Special Places in Eight Countries.* Washington D.C.: The Conservation Foundation, 1978.

Boudon, P. *Lived-in Architecture: le Corbusier's Pessac Revisited.* Cambridge, MA: MIT Press, 1972.

"Bricolage." *The Sun,* Saturday, March 14, 1987.

Brower, S. Design in familiar places: A report to the National Endowment for the Arts. Baltimore, MD: School of Social Work and Community Planning, University of Maryland at Baltimore, May 1985.

————. Planners in the neighborhood: a cautionary tale. In R. B. Taylor (ed.), *Urban Neighborhoods: Research and Policy.* New York: Praeger, 1986, pp. 181–214.

————. Territory in urban settings. In I. Altman, A. Rapoport, and J. Wohlwill (eds.), *Human Behavior and Environment, Advances in Theory and Research:* Vol. 4, *Environment and Culture.* New York: Plenum, 1980, pp. 179–207.

————. *The Design of Neighborhood Parks.* Baltimore, MD: Department of Planning, 1977a.

————. Streetfronts and backyards: two ways of looking at neighborhood open space. Baltimore, MD: Baltimore City Department of Planning, 1977b.

————. Tools, toys, masterpieces, mediums. *Landscape* 19 no. 2 (January 1975): 28–32.

————. The signs we learn to read. *Landscape* 15 no. 1 (Autumn 1965): 9–12.

Brower, S., and P. Williamson. Outdoor recreation as a function of the urban housing environment. *Environment and Behavior* 6 no. 3 (September 1974): 295–345.

Brower, S., R. B. Taylor, and S. D. Gottfredson. Responding to threat: informal social control of spaces in residential areas. In E. Pol, J. Muntanola, and M. Morales (eds.), *Man and His Environment: Qualitative Aspects.* Proceedings of the Seventh IAPS Conference. Barcelona, Spain: University of Barcelona, 1984, pp. 205–15.

Brower, S., K. Dockett, and R. B. Taylor. Residents' perception of territorial features and perceived local threat. *Environment and Behavior* 15 no. 4 (July 1983): 419–37.

Brower, S., L. Gray, and R. Stough. Doll-play as a tool for urban designers. Baltimore, MD: Baltimore City Department of Planning, August 1977.

Brower, S., R. Stough, L. Gray, and B. Headley. The design of open space for resident management. In P. Suedfeld and J. Russell (eds.), *The Behavioral Basis of Design.* Book 1: *Selected Papers.* Proceedings of the Seventh International Conference of the Environmental Design Research Association. Stroudsburg, PA: Dowden Hutchinson and Ross, 1976, pp. 275–84.

Byers, P. Cameras don't take pictures. *The Columbia University Forum* IX no. 1 (Winter 1966): 27–31.

――――. Still photography in the systematic recording and analysis of behavioral data. *Human Organization* 23 no. 1 (Spring 1964): 78–84.

Campbell, A., P. E. Converse, and W. L. Rogers. *The Quality of American Life.* New York: Russell Sage Foundation, 1976.

Canter, D. An intergroup comparison of connotative dimensions in architecture. *Environment and Behavior* 1 no. 1 (June 1969): 37–48.

――――. *The Psychology of Place.* London: The Architectural Press, 1977.

Carp, F. M., R. L. Zawadski, and H. Shokrkon. Dimensions of urban environmental quality. *Environment and Behavior* 8 no. 2 (June 1976): 239–64.

Chase, R. A. *Fairs and Festivals.* (Prepared for Baltimore City Department of Planning for inclusion in their report, A Year of Celebration.) Baltimore, MD: Department of Psychiatry and Behavioral Sciences, The Johns Hopkins University School of Medicine, 1977.

Chavis, D., P. Stucky, and A. Wandersman. Returning basic research to the community. *American Psychologist* (April 1983): 424–34.

Chein, I. The environment as a determinant of behavior. *Journal of Social Psychology* 39 (1954): 115–27.

Cherulnik, P. D., and S. K. Wilderman. Symbols of status in urban neighborhoods. *Environment and Behavior* 18 no. 5 (September 1986): 604–22.

Citizens Planning and Housing Association. *Bawlmer: An Informal Guide To A Livelier Baltimore.* Baltimore, MD: Citizens Planning and Housing Association, 1976.

Clay, G. *Close-up: How to Read the American City.* New York: Praeger, 1973.

Cooper, C. C. *Easter Hill Village: Some Social Implications of Design.* New York: The Free Press, 1975.

Cooper, C. P. Spatial and temporal patterns of tourist behavior. *Regional Studies* 15 no. 5 (1981): 359–71.

Csikszentmihalyi, M., and E. Rochberg-Halton. *The Meaning of Things: Domestic Symbols and the Self.* New York: Cambridge University Press, 1981.

Cullen, Gordon. *The Concise Townscape.* New York: van Nostrand Reinhold, 1961.

Department of the Environment. *Children at Play.* London: Her Majesty's Stationery Office, 1973.

Desai, A. The environmental perception of an urban landscape: the case of Ahmedabad. *Ekistics* 47 no. 283 (July/August 1980).

Devlin, A. S. The "small town" cognitive map: adjusting to a new environment. In G. T. Moore and R. G. Golledge (eds.), *Environmental Knowing.* Stroudsburg, PA: Dowden, Hutchinson and Ross, 1976.

de Wolfe, I. *The Italian Townscape.* New York: George Braziller, 1966.

Downs, R. M., and D. Stea. *Maps in Minds: Reflections on Cognitive Mapping.* New York: Harper and Row, 1977.

Dubos, R. *A God Within.* New York: Scribner, 1972.

DuBow, F., E. McCabe, and G. Kaplan. *Reactions to Crime: A Critical Review of the Literature.* Washington, D.C.: U.S. Department of Justice, 1979.

Eckbo, G. The landscape of tourism. *Landscape* 18 no. 2 (Spring/Summer 1969): 29–31.

Eff, E. Good screens make good neighbors: the Baltimore school of landscape artistry. In
　　D. Ward (ed.), *Personal Places: Perspectives on Informal Art Environments*. Bowling
　　Green, OH: Bowling Green State University Popular Press, 1984, pp. 15–30.

Evans, G. W., D. G. Marrero, and P. A. Butler. Environmental learning and cognitive
　　mapping. *Environment and Behavior* 13 no. 1 (1981): 83–104.

Fathy, H. *Architecture for the Poor: An Experiment in Rural Egypt*. Chicago, IL: University
　　of Chicago, 1973.

Francis, M., L. Cashdan, and L. Paxson. *Community Open Spaces*. Washington, D.C.:
　　Island Press, 1984.

Fried, M. Residential attachment: sources of residential and community satisfaction.
　　Journal of Social Issues 38 no. 3 (1982): 107–19.

Galster, G. C., and G. W. Hesser. Residential satisfaction: compositional and con-
　　textual correlates. *Environment and Behavior* 13 no. 6 (November 1981): 735–58.

Gans, H. J. *The Levittowners: Ways of Life and Politics in a New Suburban Community*.
　　New York: Pantheon Books, 1967.

―――――. *People and Plans*. New York: Basic Books, 1968.

―――――. *The Urban Villagers: Group and Class in the Life of Italian Americans*. New York:
　　The Free Press, 1962.

Geertz, C., H. Geertz, and L. Rosen. *Meaning and Order in Moroccan Society*. New York:
　　Cambridge University Press, 1979.

Gibberd, F. *Town Design*. London: The Architectural Press, 1953.

Gold, S. R. Neighborhood parks: the nonuse phenomenon. *Evaluation Quarterly* 1 no. 2
　　(May 1977): 319–28.

Gorman, M., et al. (eds.). *Design for Tourism: An ICSID Interdesign Report*. New York:
　　Pergamon, 1977.

Gould, P., and R. White. *Mental Maps*. Baltimore, MD: Penguin, 1974.

Grahame, K. *The Wind in the Willows*. New York: Scribner, 1961.

Gray, L., and S. Brower. Activities of children in an urban neighborhood. Baltimore,
　　MD: Department of Planning, August, 1977 (monograph).

Gregory, R. L. *The Intelligent Eye*. New York: McGraw Hill, 1970.

―――――. Visual illusions. *Scientific American* (November 1968). Reprinted in *Perception:
　　Mechanisms and Models* (a series of readings from *Scientific American*). San Francis-
　　co: W. H. Freeman, n.d., pp. 241–51.

Grigsby, W. G., and L. Rosenberg. *Urban Housing Policy*. New Brunswick, NJ: Transac-
　　tion Books, 1975.

Gruen, V. *The Heart of Our Cities: The Urban Crisis, Diagnosis and Cure*. New York:
　　Simon and Schuster, 1964.

Hanson, J., and B. Hillier. Domestic space organisation: two contemporary space codes
　　compared. *Architecture and Behavior* 2 (1982): 5–25.

Harrison, J., and P. Sarre. Personal construct theory in the measurement of environmen-
　　tal images: problems and methods. *Environment and Behavior* 3 no. 4 (December
　　1971): 351–74.

Hatch, R. (ed.). *The Scope of Social Architecture*. New York: Van Nostrand Reinhold,
　　1984.

Heinig, J., and M. G. Maxfield. Reducing fear of crime: strategies for intervention.
　　Victimology: An International Journal 3 nos. 3–4 (1978): 279–313.

Heinzelmann, F. Crime prevention and the physical environment. In D. A. Lewis (ed.),
　　Reactions to Crime. Beverly Hills, CA: Sage, 1981, pp. 87–101.

Hershberger, R. G. Predicting the meaning of designed environments. Paper presented at the Western Psychological Association Meeting, San Francisco, April 24, 1971.

Hinderlang, M. J., M. R. Gottfredson, and J. Garofalo. *Victims of Personal Crime: An Empirical Foundation for a Theory of Personal Victimization.* Cambridge, MA: Ballinger, 1978.

Hinshaw, M., and K. Allott. Environmental preferences of future housing consumers. *Journal of the American Institute of Planners* 38 no. 2 (March 1972): 102–7.

Howe, E. Role choices of urban planners. *Journal of the American Planning Association* 46 (October 1980): 394–409.

Hudson, R. Patterns of spatial search. *Transactions, The Institute of British Geographers* 65 (July 1975): 141–54.

Huizinga, J. *Homo Ludens: A Study of the Play-Element in Culture.* Boston: Beacon Press, 1955.

Hunter, A. *Symbolic Communities.* Chicago: University of Chicago Press, 1974.

————. Symbols of incivility: social disorder and fear of crime in urban neighborhoods. Paper presented at the annual meeting of the American Society of Criminology, Dallas, 1978.

Imamoglu, V. Assessment of living rooms by householders and architects. In J. G. Simon (ed.), *Conflicting Experiences of Space.* Louvain-la-Neuve, Belgium, 1979. Also appears as Research Report no. 1, Ankara, Turkey: Middle-East Technical University, Department of Building Science and Environmental Design.

Jackson, J. B. *The Necessity for Ruins, and Other Topics.* Amherst, MA: University of Massachusetts Press, 1980.

James, W. *The Principles of Psychology.* New York: Dover Publications, 1950.

Kaplan, S., F. D. Dale, and R. Kaplan. Patterns as hypotheses: an empirical test. In J. Harvey and D. Henning (eds.), *Public Environments.* Proceedings of the Eighteenth Environmental Design Research Association Conference. Washington, D.C.: Environmental Design Research Association, 1987, pp. 188–93.

Kaplan, S., and R. Kaplan. *Cognition and Environment: Functioning in an Uncertain World.* New York: Praeger, 1982.

Keller, S. *The Urban Neighborhood: A Sociological Perspective.* New York: Random House, 1968.

Kelly, G. A. *The Psychology of Personal Constructs.* New York: W. W. Norton, 1955.

Kendall/Hunt Publishing Co. Press release for "Architecture and Applied Design: An Environmental Design Perspective" by Anthony C. Antoniades. Dubuque, IO: Kendall/Hunt, 1980.

Koffka, K. *Principles of Gestalt Psychology.* New York: Harcourt Brace, 1935.

Korten, D. Community organization and rural development: a learning process approach. *Public Administration Review* (Sept./Oct. 1980): 480–511.

Kron, J. *Home-Psych: The Social Psychology of Home and Decoration.* New York: Clarkson N. Potter, 1983.

Lamanna, R. A. Value consensus among urban residents. *Journal of the American Institute of Planners* 30 no. 4 (November 1964): 317–22.

Lansing, J. B. and R. W. Marans. Evaluation of neighborhood quality. *Journal of the American Institute of Planners* (May 1969): 195–99.

le Corbusier. *Towards a New Architecture* (translated from the thirteenth French edition by Frederick Etchells). New York: Brewer, Warren and Putnam Inc.. n.d.

————. *The City of Tomorrow.* Cambridge, MA: MIT Press, 1971.

Lee, T. Psychology and living space. In R. M. Downs and D. Stea (eds.), *Image and Environment: Cognitive Mapping and Spatial Behavior.* Chicago: Aldine Publishing, 1973, pp. 87–108.

Lewis, D. A. and M. G. Maxfield. Fear in the neighborhoods: an investigation of the impact of crime. *Journal of Research in Crime and Delinquency* 17 no. 2 (July 1980): 160–89.

Lewis, P. F. Common houses, cultural spoors. *Landscape* 19 no. 2 (January 1975): 1–22.

Lofland, L. H. *A World of Strangers: Order and Action in Urban Public Space.* New York: Basic Books, 1973.

Loos, A. *Gentlemen Prefer Blondes.* New York: Curtis Books, 1963.

Lowenthal, D. The American scene. *Geographical Review* 58 (1968): 61–88.

———. Past time, present place: landscape and memory. *Geographical Review* 65 no. 1 (1975): 1–36.

Lynch, K. *The Image of the City.* Cambridge, MA: MIT Press, 1960.

———. *A Theory of Good City Form.* Cambridge, MA: MIT Press, 1981.

Lyons, E. Demographic correlates of landscape preference. *Environment and Behavior* 15 no. 4 (July 1983): 487–511.

MacCannell, D. *The Tourist: A New Theory of the Leisure Class.* New York: Schocken, 1976.

———. Staged Authenticity: arrangements of social space in tourist settings. *American Journal of Sociology* 79 no. 1 (1973): 589–603.

Maurios, G. The limits of flexibility. In C. R. Hatch (ed.), *The Scope of Social Architecture.* New York: Van Nostrand Reinhold, 1984, pp. 65–75.

Meier, R. L. *Urban Futures Observed in the Asian Third World.* New York: Pergamon, 1980.

Meinig, D. W. (ed.), *The Interpretation of Ordinary Landscapes: Geographical Essays.* New York: Oxford University Press, 1979.

Michelson, W. *Man and His Urban Environment: A Sociological Approach* (with revisions). Reading, MA: Addison-Wesley, 1976.

Milgrim, S. The experience of living in cities. *Science* 167 no. 3924 (March 13, 1970): 1461–68.

Miller, F. D., S. Tsemberis, G. P. Malia, and D. Grega. Neighborhood satisfaction among urban dwellers. *Journal of Social Issues* 36 no. 3 (1980): 101–17.

Mitford, N. The tourist. *Encounter* 13 no. 4 (October 1959): 3–7.

Moore, C., G. Allen, and D. Lyndon. *The Place of Houses.* New York: Holt, Rinehart and Winston, 1974.

Mortimer, J. Rumpole and the genuine article, in *Rumpole and the Golden Thread.* New York: Viking Penguin, 1984.

Munson, B. E. Attitudes toward urban and suburban residence in Indianapolis. *Social Forces* 35 (1956): 76–80.

Nasar, J. L. Adult viewers' preferences in residential scenes: a study of the relationship of environmental attributes to preference. *Environment and Behavior* 15 no. 5 (September 1983): 589–614.

Nasar, J. L., and C. Kunawong. Architect and lay judgments of architecture: do they really differ? In J. Harvey and D. Henning (eds.), *Public Environments.* Proceedings of the Eighteenth Environmental Design Research Association Conference. Washington, D.C.: Environmental Design Research Association, 1987, pp. 205–10.

Nash, D. Tourism as a form of imperialism. In Valene L. Smith (ed.), *Hosts and Guests: The Anthropology of Tourism*. Philadelphia, PA: University of Pennsylvania Press, 1977.

Nassauer, J., and R. Westmacott. Progressiveness as an ideal among farmers as a factor in disturbance and loss of heterogeneity in farmed landscapes. Paper presented at Landscape Ecology Conference, sponsored by the Institute of Ecology at the University of Georgia, Athens, Georgia, 1985.

Newman, O. *Defensible Space: Crime Prevention Through Urban Design*. New York: Mac-Millan, 1973.

_____. *Community of Interest*. Garden City, NY: Anchor, 1980.

Norberg-Schulz, C. *Meaning in Western Architecture*. New York: Rizzoli, 1980.

Palmer, J. Residential greenspace visual quality. Presented at workshop on environmental meaning: the problem of contextual fit, Fourteenth International Conference of the Environmental Design Research Association, Lincoln, Nebraska, 1983.

Pearce, P. L. *The Social Psychology of Tourist Behavior*. New York: Pergamon, 1982.

Peterson, G. L. A model of preference: quantitative analysis of the perception of the visual appearance of residential neighborhoods. *Journal of Regional Science* 7 no. 1 (1967): 19–31.

Rainwater, L. Fear and the house-as-haven in the lower class. *Journal of the American Institute of Planners* 32 no. 1 (January 1966): 23–31.

Rapoport, A. *Human Aspects of Urban Form: Towards a Man–Environment Approach to Urban Form and Design*. New York: Pergamon, 1977.

_____. *The Meaning of the Built Environment: A Nonverbal Communication Approach*. Beverly Hills, CA: Sage, 1982.

Robinson and Associates. Street games children play: a primer on inner-city recreation. Report to the Department of Planning, Baltimore, MD, May 1977.

Rosen, B. F. Design criteria for hi-rise living for the elderly. Report prepared for the Baltimore City Department of Housing and Community Development, August 1971 (mimeo).

Sanoff, H. *Designing with Community Participation*. Stroudsburg, PA: Hutchinson Ross, 1978.

Seaton, R. W., and J. B. Collins. Validity and reliability of ratings of simulated buildings. In *Environmental Design: Research and Practice*, Proceedings of the Third Environmental Design Research Association Conference. Los Angeles, CA: Regents of the University of California, 1972, pp. 6.10.1–6.10.12.

Shafer, E. L. Jr., and T. A. Richards. A comparison of viewer reactions to outdoor scenes and photographs of those scenes. In D. Canter and T. Lee (eds.), *Psychology and the Built Environment*. New York: John Wiley, 1974, 71–79.

Shafer, E. L. Jr., J. F. Hamilton, and E. A. Schmidt. Natural landscape preferences: a predictive model. *Journal of Leisure Research* 1 nos. 1–19 (1969).

Simkin, C. (ed.). *A Currier and Ives Treasury*. New York: Crown, 1955.

Sitte, C. *The Art of Building Cities: City Building According to its Artistic Foundations*. New York: Reinhold, 1945.

Sitwell, O. *Miracle on Sinai: A Satirical Novel*. London: Duckworth, 1933.

Smith, V. L. (ed.). *Hosts and Guests: The Anthropology of Tourism*. Philadelphia, PA: University of Pennsylvania Press, 1977.

Sommer, R. Action research is not business as usual. In D. Duerk and D. Campbell (eds.), *The Challenge of Diversity*. Proceedings of the Fifteenth Environmental

Design Research Association Conference. Washington, D.C.: Environmental Design Research Association, 1984, pp. 3–8.

Steele, F. *The Sense of Place.* Boston, MA: CBI Publishing Co., 1981.

Taylor, R. B. Results of the Harlem Park innovation project survey. Baltimore, MD: Center for Metropolitan Planning and Research, The Johns Hopkins University, November 1983.

Taylor, R. B., and S. Brower. Home and near-home territories. In I. Altman and C. Werner (eds.), *Home Environment: Advances in Theory and Research.* New York: Plenum, 1985, pp. 183–212.

Taylor, R. B., S. D. Gottfredson, and S. Brower. Understanding block crime and fear. *Journal of Research in Crime and Delinquency* 21 (1984): 303–31.

――――. Informal control in the urban residential environment (final report). Baltimore, MD: Center for Metropolitan Planning and Research, The Johns Hopkins University, 1981a.

――――. Territorial cognitions and social climate in urban neighborhoods. *Basic and Applied Psychology* 2 (1981b): 289–303.

――――. Informal control in the urban residential environment (draft report). Baltimore, MD: Center for Metropolitan Planning and Research, The Johns Hopkins University, September 1980.

Taylor, R. B., S. Brower, and R. Stough. User-generated visual features as signs in the urban residential environment. In P. Suedfeld and J. Russell (eds.), *The Behavioral Basis of Design.* Book 1: *Selected Papers.* Proceedings of the Seventh International Conference of the Environmental Design Research Association. Stroudsburg, PA: Dowden Hutchinson and Ross, 1976, pp. 94–101.

Thompson, M. *Rubbish Theory: The Creation and Destruction of Value.* New York: Oxford University Press, 1979.

Troy, P. N. Residents and their preferences: property prices and residential quality. *Regional Studies,* vol. 7. Great Britain: Pergamon, 1973, pp. 183–92.

Twain, M. *Life on the Mississippi.* New York: Harper, 1929.

Tyler, A. *Dinner at the Homesick Restaurant.* New York: Alfred A. Knopf, 1982.

Ugly Is Beautiful: The Main Street School of Architecture. *Atlantic Monthly,* May 1973, pp. 33–43.

U.S. Department of Commerce. *Creating Economic Growth and Jobs through Travel and Tourism.* Washington, D.C.: U.S. Government Printing Office, February 1970.

Violich, F. *An Experiment in Revealing The Sense of Place: A Subjective Reading of Six Dalmatian Towns.* Berkeley, CA: Center for Environmental Design Research, University of California, Berkeley, January 1983.

Wagner, J. (ed.). *Images of Information: Still Photography in the Social Sciences.* Beverly Hills, CA: Sage, 1979, pp. 147–59, 161–69.

Ward, C. *The Child in the City.* New York: Pantheon, 1978.

Warren, D. I. *The Health of American Neighborhoods: A National Report.* Anne Arbor, MI: Community Effectiveness Institute, November 1982.

Wartofsky, M. W. Cameras can't see: representation, photography and human vision. *Photo Communique* 2 no. 1 (March/April 1980): 2–4.

Wilmott, P. *The Evolution of a Community.* London: Routledge and Kegan Paul, 1963.

Wilson, R. L. Livability of the city: attitudes and urban development. In F. S. Chapin, Jr. and S. F. Weiss (eds.), *Urban Growth Dynamics in a Regional Cluster of Cities.* New York: Wiley, 1962, pp. 359–99.

Winkel, G. H. The perception of neighborhood change. In J. Harvey (ed.), *Cognition, Social Behavior and the Environment.* Hillsdale, NJ: Laurence Erlbaum Associates, 1981.

Wolfe, T. *The Painted Word.* New York: Farrar, Straus and Giroux, 1975.

Zajonc, R. B. Attitudinal effects of mere exposure. *Journal of Personality and Social Psychology Monograph Supplement* 9 no. 2, part 2 (June 1968).

Zube, E. H. Cross-disciplinary and intermode agreement on the description and evaluation of landscape resources. *Environment and Behavior* 6 no. 1 (March 1974): 69–89.

———— (ed.). *Landscapes: Selected Writings of J. B. Jackson.* Amherst, MA: University of Massachusetts Press, 1970.

Index

ABOUT THE AUTHOR

SIDNEY BROWER was born in South Africa. He studied architecture at the University of Cape Town and city planning at the Massachusetts Institute of Technology. He was chief of Comprehensive Planning and chief of Design Analysis in the Baltimore City Department of Planning where, with the assistance of federal grants, he studied residents' and visitors' perceptions and use of the city, and applied the findings to the development of design guidelines. He has published many journal articles and has contributed to several books. He has taught at Johns Hopkins University, and is now associate professor in the Community Planning Program of the University of Maryland at Baltimore.